Generis
PUBLISHING

Valuation of Companies: Core Issues and Critical Perspective

Tajana Serdar Raković

Title: **Valuation of Companies:**
Core Issues and Critical Perspective

ISBN: 979-8-89966-236-2

Author: Tajana Serdar Raković

Cover image: Tajana Serdar Raković

Publisher: Generis Publishing
Online orders: www.generis-publishing.com
Contact email: info@generis-publishing.com

VALUATION OF COMPANIES: CORE ISSUES AND CRITICAL PERSPECTIVE

Tajana Serdar Raković, PhD, Associate Professor, University of Banja Luka Faculty of Economics, Bosnia and Herzegovina, tajana.serdar-rakovic@ef.unibl.org

Preface to the Volume: Tracing a Decade of Inquiry

This book brings together a curated selection of academic works written between 2015 and 2024, unified by a common focus: the complexity of company valuation in developing and illiquid capital markets. Each chapter explores critical dimensions of valuation: discount rates, country risk, market liquidity, start-up uncertainties, and methodological adjustments, through both theoretical and applied lenses.

Where appropriate, literature reviews, conceptual frameworks, and theoretical discussions have been revised and expanded to reflect developments up to 2025. This ensures that the collection remains a relevant and rigorous resource for students, practitioners, and researchers alike.

While the editing process allowed for theoretical updates, I have chosen to preserve the original methodological and empirical frameworks of each study to maintain contextual and chronological integrity. Empirical sections retain their original data, sample periods, and methodological assumptions. This decision supports full transparency regarding the conditions under which the research was conducted and offers a clearer understanding of how real-world circumstances have evolved alongside academic approaches.

By presenting these works as a continuous intellectual journey rather than a single, time-frozen study, the collection honors both the progress and persistence of core valuation challenges in transitional economies. Readers may thus encounter a natural temporal layering, where empirical evidence reflects earlier realities, while theoretical insights have been refined to engage with contemporary discourse.

I remain grateful to the editors and the publishing team for their support of this collection, and I hope it will serve as a meaningful contribution to ongoing discussions in corporate finance and valuation.

With appreciation,

Tajana Serdar Raković

Banja Luka, October 2025.

CONTENTS

I [*]DISCOUNT RATE PROBLEMS: WHEN SHOULD COUNTRY RISK BE INCLUDED IN THE DISCOUNT RATE?

Abstract

According to the globalization of the world economy and economic growth, capital markets of developing countries are developing, but the biggest concern in the valuation of companies from these markets is based precisely on the assessment of country risk, which can often overcome the risk of the company. The unstable local currencies, lack of transparency and lack of key information entailed in valuation, poor corporate governance and country risk in developing/inactive capital markets withdraw considerable uncertainties in the company valuation. The answer to the question whether it is necessary to include country risk in the calculation of key parameters, in this case, the discount rate, depends on the characteristics of the company. The first group of companies in this regard, are those operating solely on the domestic market when the country risk is not involved. The other extreme when there will be no country risk premium is in the case of possibility of full diversification of country risk (which is unlikely in practice). In all other cases, the companies that lie down on the scale between these two extremes, it is necessary to include country risk in the calculation of discount rate. The aim of the research is to explain the method of determining country risk, its impact on the discount rate and the importance of country risk for a realistic and relevant valuation of company value viewed from an international perspective.

Keywords: *discount rate, country risk, beta, lambda, developing capital market*

---

[*] *Originally published in 2016 in the Journal Financing,), 7(4), pp. 37–45. Reused here with permission from the publisher.*

INTRODUCTION

With the globalization of the world economy and the rapid development of economies in Asia, Latin America, and the rest of the world, in the last 20 years or so, new financial markets have developed. In line with economic growth, the capital markets of developing countries are also developing. An increasing number of companies listed on developing capital markets are becoming major players in the global economy, and the biggest preoccupation in the assessment of these companies is based precisely on the assessment of the country's risk, which often exceeds the risk of the company itself. Namely, unstable currency and inflation, variations in the accounting practices of application of IAS/IFSI and rules of corporate governance in developing countries result in a lack of transparency in the matter of current earnings and investments, which raises considerable doubts in the assessment. Also, even with very promising companies, it is difficult to estimate growth if the entire capital market is in crisis. Therefore, the country risk that is added to the company risk must somehow be included in the calculation of the discount rate in the valuations of the companies listed on the emerging/inactive capital markets.

The need to evaluate companies listed on emerging capital markets becomes more important as these markets grow and become more sophisticated. Many of the companies from developing countries have securities listed on the stock exchanges in London and New York in order to overcome the problems characteristic of underdeveloped capital markets and attract global investors. The basic characteristics of companies from the developing capital market are as follows:

- *Currency volatility*. In many developing countries, exchange rate volatility and inflation occur. The absence of a long-term interest rate on bonds without execution risk in the domestic currency makes it impossible to calculate the risk-free rate.
- *Country risk*. The growth of developing countries is accompanied by macroeconomic risks. The success of a company depends not only on its performance and business decisions, but also on the political and economic situation in a given country.
- *Unreliable market measures*. In developing capital markets, measures such as market indices and stock returns are less useful if the capital market is illiquid and if companies mostly borrow money from banks (rather than issue bonds).

- *Information gap and differences in accounting practices*. It is not uncommon for companies in emerging capital markets to withhold significant information about earnings, reinvestment and debt, despite increasingly stringent financial disclosure requirements globally.
- *Corporate governance*. The question of the power relationship between shareholders and managers is particularly interesting because a large number of enterprises in developing countries have developed from family businesses. In such cases, management is more difficult to change than in developed capital markets, both due to legal restrictions and the inability to access capital.
- *Discontinuous risk*. In addition to country risk, which contributes to volatility in emerging capital markets, additional risk, although unlikely, appears in the form of looming nationalization and terrorism.

In the process of calculating the valuation parameters, the question arises whether to include country risk in the calculation of the discount rate or possibly cash flows. In professional and scientific literature, the prevailing view is that country risk should be taken into account in the calculation of key parameters, in this case the discount rate, in all cases when a company enters the international market. When a company operates on the global market, its suppliers, customers, creditors, business partners and others will observe the foreign company from their (international) perspective and carefully analyse the situation in the country where the given company is headquartered. Therefore, the key determinant in the valuation of companies in developing capital markets is the discount rate, which must be theoretically and empirically consistent with the definition of the discounted economic return. Due to the non-transparency of information and the lack of key inputs for determining the discount rate, and other inherent risks, this valuation parameter is very problematic for determining in developing capital markets, such as the capital market of Bosnia and Herzegovina.

The goal of the research is to explain the method of determining country risk, its impact on the discount rate, and the importance of country risk for a realistic and relevant assessment of the value of a company from an international perspective. In order to prove the claims, we will refer to the concept of discount rate, the method of calculating beta as a measure of systematic risk, and process the most important models for determining the cost of own capital. At the end of the paper, a part of the empirical research related to the topic of the discount rate is presented and concluding considerations are given.

1. CONCEPT OF DISCOUNT RATE

The discount rate represents the cost of capital that reflects the level of riskiness of the investment. Unlike the discount rate, the capitalization rate represents the denominator of a fraction whose numerator is a certain economic income (e.g. earnings or cash flow). Only if the expected level of economic income were constant over an infinite period would these two rates be equal. The discount rate depends on three types of risk (Mikerević, 2009, p. 200):

- **Business risk**, which is divided into systematic or market (inevitable) and unsystematic or corporate (influenced by the characteristics of the company);
- **Financial risk**, associated with financing;
- **Total risk**, which consists of company-specific risk and market risk (product of business and financial risk).

When cash flow after debt servicing is used, the discount rate represents the cost of own capital, and with cash flow before debt servicing, it is the required rate of return on total capital, i.e. WACC (Weighted Average Cost of Capital). Regarding the concept of fair market value, the discount rate is derived from the market, and represents the expected total yield rate or rate of return required for investors to accept investing in the asset, taking into account its level of risk. The discount rate consists of the following elements:

1) **Risk-free rates** that include: the rate of rent for the use of funds and the expected rate of inflation during that period. This rate refers to instruments that are assumed not to carry the risk of default (e.g. short-term government bonds);

2) **Risk premiums**, which include: *systematic risk* (related to the return on investments on the market) and *unsystematic risk* (risk specific to the investment in question). The risk premium contains three subcomponents:

- the ownership risk premium;
- the small business premium;
- the business-specific risk premium.

The discount rate sometimes includes other characteristics: the level of minority versus controlling interest and the level of marketability or lack of marketability. As the cost of capital is one of the most important variables in valuation, theorists as well as practitioners have devoted enormous effort to research in an attempt to quantify the effects of risk on the cost of equity capital. The discount rate can be further broken down into several factors that reflect risk (Pratt & Grabowski, 2008):

1) Basic risk premium (added to the risk-free rate of return);
2) Coefficients that modify the basic risk premium, based on the characteristics of the economic branch or other characteristics that reflect the level of investment risk;
3) An element that reflects the effect of size;
4) Final adjustment for unsystematic risk not included in the first three categories. While there is empirical research and evidence for the first three factors, the last factor is subject to the subjective assessment of the analyst.

Beta as a measure of systematic risk

Systematic risk is the uncertainty of future returns arising from the sensitivity of the returns of a given investment to the movements of returns on the investment market as a whole. Unsystematic risk is a function of the characteristics of the investment, the individual firm, or the type of investment interest (Pratt & Grabowski, 2008). Beta is a measure of future risk and is a function of the excess of the expected return on the HOV in relation to the excess of the expected return on the market index (Meitner & Streitferdt, 2014). For the market index as a whole, beta is equal to 1. If the difference between the return on the stock and the risk-free return is greater than the difference between the market return and the risk-free return, the company will have a beta greater than 1 (otherwise it is less than 1).

Beta measures the volatility of an individual stock's excess return relative to the market return. In general, stocks with a beta greater than 1 are more aggressive and risky, and those with a beta less than 1 are defensive and less risky. The basic assumption of the CAPM is that the share of the risk premium in the expected return on the HOV is a function of the systematic risk of the HOV. Beta can also be negative, and in this case it shows that such a share has countercyclical returns with the returns of broader investments in the market index. Beta is calculated in three ways.

1) *Historical price data*. Beta is determined using data from large corporations, which are, in essence, assessment services: Merrill, Value Line, Standard & Poor's, Morningstar, Bloomberg, etc. Factors that influence the calculation of beta are: the length of the valuation period (data for 2-5 years), the return period of the stock

(daily, monthly, and weekly) and the market index (the index of the market in which the shares are traded).

Beta estimates for emerging markets proceed in the same way, but the choice of return period and market index differs. When liquidity is reduced, estimated betas with a short return interval are biased. Using daily and weekly data will lead to betas that are not good measures of a company's actual market risk. In developing markets, both companies and the market change significantly in a short period of time. Return data over, say, five years may bear little resemblance to the company and market now. Market measures of returns in many small, inactive and emerging markets tend to be dominated by a few large firms. When the market index is dominated by one or several companies, the beta estimated by that index does not reflect the true measure of market risk (eg the Brazilian index Bovespa or the German stock index DAX - Deutscher Aktienindex). Beta will then be high quality for a large company and significantly variable for everyone else. Historical betas will be too skewed or biased in the valuation process to be meaningful measures of the firm's equity risk.

2) *Basic characteristics of the investment (fundamental beta).* They are calculated through regression analysis (Damodaran, 2012), where it is necessary to know:

    - What type of business the company performs - the more sensitive the business is to market conditions, the higher the beta;
    - What is the business (operating) leverage used in the company - the higher the fixed costs, the higher the business leverage, the greater the variability of the business profit, and thus the beta for that company is higher;
    - What is the company's financial leverage - an increase in financial leverage with other unchanged variables leads to an increase in the beta of the share.

    This separation of the components of business risk and financial leverage contributed to the calculation of beta, which does not have to be based on the data of individual companies - the beta of building from the bottom to the top (Bottom-up Beta). The possibility of predicting future returns based on market movements, especially in developed markets, has been established in several studies (Bhattacharya & Bhattacharya, 2013).

3) *Accounting earnings* as a third way of determining beta. Changes in earnings on a quarterly or annual basis are associated with changes in earnings on the market in the same period, resulting in accounting beta. The problem with this approach is the fact that the accounting earnings that are settled in relation to the value of the

company are estimated at one point in time, because the costs and revenues are recorded throughout the period. This leads to unreliable downward beta for riskier and higher beta for less risky firms (Meitner & Streitferdt, 2014). Accounting earnings may be influenced by non-operating factors such as changes in depreciation or inventory management methods or the allocation of costs from the parent company to subsidiaries. Finally, accounting earnings are usually measured annually and at most quarterly in regression analysis, leading to several conclusions without greater explanatory power (high standard errors and low R square).

What method of determining beta to use? Accounting earnings can be misleading, and historical prices for individual companies are critical due to standard errors of estimation, the lack of local indices (in developing capital markets) and the inability of regression analysis to reflect the effects of major changes in the company's business and financial leverage. This is particularly important from the aspect of investment analysis and assessment. Furthermore, by eliminating the need for historical stock prices, the standard error in the regression analysis is reduced relative to the betas of individual companies. Bottom-up betas are based on the average betas of a large number of companies from the economic sector, which covers all the problems related to the calculation of the cost of capital and has proven to be particularly useful in determining the cost of capital of growing stocks. Beta represents the basis of the most commonly used model for determining the cost of own capital - CAPM.

2. MODELS FOR DETERMINING THE COST OF EQUITY

Depending on the combination of key elements, there are several models for determining the cost of equity: the Build-up model, the CAPM, the APT (Arbitrage Pricing Theory) Model, the Fama-French Three-factor Model, and the Dividend Discounting Model. The most common are the build-up model –and the CAPM, and they are the subject of a more detailed analysis.

2.1. Build-up Model

The cost of capital according to the build-up model is the sum of two components: *the risk-free rate* and the risk premium, which includes three subcomponents: the general market risk premium, the size risk premium (for small companies) and the company-specific risk premium. It may also include a country risk premium as a result of uncertainty due to political and economic instability in the country (Pratt & Grabowski, 2008, p. 70).

$$E(R_i) = R_f + RP_m + RP_s + RP_u$$

where $E(_{Ri})$ is the expected rate of return on the share (cost of capital), R_f is the risk-free rate of return, RP_m is the equity risk premium, Rp_s is the premium for risk of a smaller size, PR_u is the premium for risk specific to the company or the economic branch (unsystematic risk).

The difference between this formula and the extended CAPM is the omission of beta. The first three components are the same as in the CAPM: the risk-free rate, the market risk premium, and the size risk premium. The value of the company-specific risk premium is slightly different, because the beta in the CAPM already includes some of the company-specific risks. The company specificity premium reflects company characteristics that may be higher or lower than typical companies of the same size and from the same market. Company-specific adjustments include an analysis of five factors: size that is less than the smallest size premium in the group, industry risk, return volatility, financial leverage and other specific factors.

A size that is smaller than the smallest size premium in the group implies an adjustment to the expected return. Unlike the extended CAPM, which only includes a size premium, the bricklaying model incorporates both that premium and an additional factor for the smallest stocks covered by specific risks.

Risk of the industry (industrial risk). An alternative formula for the build-up model, where the industry risk premium (RPi) is added, is used by Morningstar:

$$E(R_i) = R_f + RP_m + RP_s \pm RP_i + RP_u$$

where RP_i is the risk of the economic branch.

The industry in which the company operates can be more or less risky compared to the average of other companies of the same size. Although this factor is difficult to measure, in case the company belongs to an extremely risk-free or high-risk branch, the expected rate of return will be adjusted downwards or upwards.

Return volatility is expressed via standard deviation. High return volatility is an additional risk factor and it corrects the expected return.

Financial leverage. A capital structure that deviates significantly from the average capital structure in the branch requires adjustments to the expected return, where higher leverage leads to the determination of a higher cost of own capital.

Other company-specific factors. The rate of risk of investing in a given country derives from the amount of risk associated with the assets, the risk of the business environment and the financial risk. On the other hand, the risk rate of investing in a company includes a gradation of elements, that is, the type of risk that is carried out according to the following components (Mikerević, 2009; Pratt & Grabowski, 2008): dependence on a key person, dependence on a key supplier, unusual current or possible competition, strength or management weakness, pending regulatory changes, pending litigation, product and geographic diversification, diversification and customer concentration, predictability, etc.

In addition to the similarity in determining the variables, the build-up model shares with the CAPM the highest degree of use in practical calculations of the cost of equity capital.

2.2. CAPM (Capital Asset Pricing Model)

CAPM is the cornerstone of modern capital market theory. Its importance for assessment is that the company represents one of the possible investment opportunities on the capital market, and therefore the price of the company's capital should be viewed according to the same economic principles that regulate the prices of other investment assets. The general formula of the CAPM reads (Pratt & Grabowski, 2008, p. 81):

$$E(R_i) = R_f + \beta(RP_m)$$

where: $E(R_i)$ – expected return on share i, R_f – rate of return on risk-free HOV or risk-free rate, β - beta, RPm - premium for ownership risk for the market as a whole (premium for ownership risk for HOV with β = 1) or market risk premium (ERP).

The risk-free rate represents the rate of return on a 20-year, 10-year, 5-year government bond or a 30-day Treasury note available on the valuation date. As the first component in the CAPM, it contains three elements:

- rent rate (actual return on capital investment during the investment period);
- inflation rate (expected);
- maturity risk or investment rate risk. Investment rate risk is the risk of growth or decline in value in the period until maturity due to changes in the general level of interest rates.

Since the risk-free rate includes inflation, the cash flows on which the process of determining the cost of capital is based should be expressed in nominal amounts (Cai, Chlacher & Keasey, 2013). The risk-free rate in developed countries ranges from 1-6%. The risk-free rate for companies in emerging capital markets can be determined in three ways.

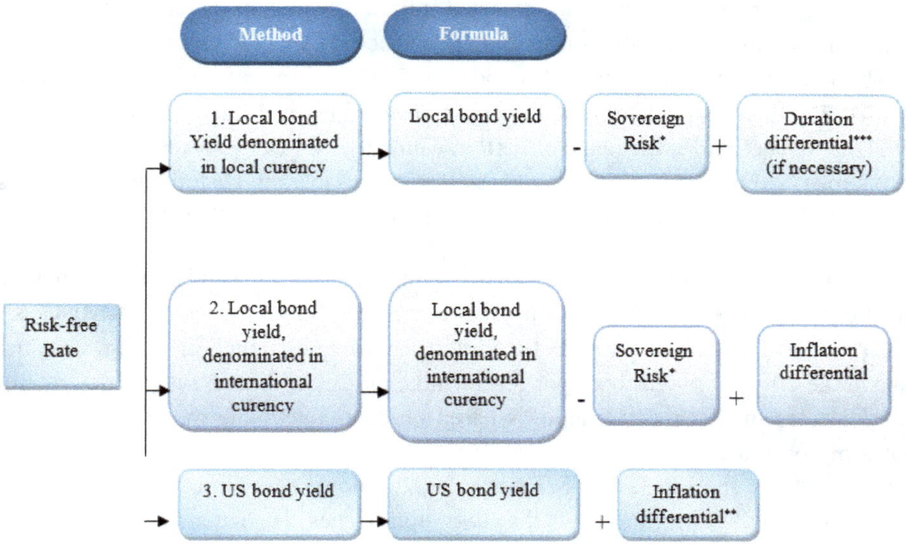

Chart 1: Calculating the Risk-Free Rate in the Emerging Capital Market

*The sovereign risk premium is the difference between the yield on a domestic bond denominated in US dollars and a US government bond of equal maturity (including both country and credit risk).

** The difference between the domestic inflation rate and the US inflation rate over 10 years.

*** Change in yield between bonds with different maturities.

Source: Copeland, Koller & Murrin, 2000, p. 387.

The choice of method depends on which bond is available and liquid. If possible, it is useful to determine the risk-free rate by all three methods. A key assumption is that investors have access to an international risk-free rate, on the basis of which the same rate is fairly easily arrived at in the developing capital market (Pereiro, 2006).

Equity Risk Premium (ERP) or market risk premium (for equity) reflects systematic risk and is defined as the difference between the expected return on a fully diversified stock portfolio and the risk-free rate:

$$RP_m = R_m - R_f$$

where: RP_m – market risk premium, R_m – expected return on a fully diversified stock portfolio and R_f – rate of return on risk-free HOV.

R_f and R_m can be nominal (with expected inflation included) or real (with expected inflation excluded), but inflation should not affect the expected rate of return (Pratt & Grabowski, 2008). According to Damodaran (2012), the market risk premium ranges from 4-5% on average (determined by comparison with government bond rates). Koller et al. (2010) determine the range of ERP movement at 4.5-5.5%, while Brealey, Myers & Marcus (2011) extend the range to 5-8% for the US market. Historically, market risk premium hovered between 5.3 and 5.7 percent in period 2011-2024 (Statista, 2024).

The market risk premium can be calculated using historical data and premiums realized in previous periods. Historical returns are available in the Ibbotson SBBI Classic Yearbook as well as the Duff&Phelps editions, and are based on S&P 500 stock returns above the 20-year, 5-year bond, or 30-day note returns . Another way of determining the expected market risk premium is based on data concerning the expected growth rates of corporate earnings or dividends or from projections of dividends and future prices made by analysts (Fama & French, 2002; Salomons & Grootveld, 2003). There is no unified view which of the two approaches is better in terms of the representativeness of current premiums.

Another version of the CAPM includes an extension of the original model by including a premium for firm size and a premium for specific ownership risk. The extended CAPM reads (Pratt & Grabowski, 2008):

$$E(R_i) = R_f + \beta(RP_m) + RP_s + RP_u$$

where: R_f – risk-free rate, RP_m – market risk premium, RP_s – premium for the risk of small company size, Rp_u – premium for risk attributable to the specifics of the company (premium for unsystematic risk).

The size risk premium reflects additional returns on stocks of companies smaller than those in the market index (in the US smaller than the S&P 500). Includes an additional return of 10% of the smallest withdrawals on the stock market. Many studies show that small businesses have a higher rate of return than large ones. Total risk and standard deviation of annual returns increase as firm size decreases. In the CAPM, systematic risk and beta risk are included, and small firms have higher returns than their betas imply. Therefore, the market does not ignore the unsystematic risk of smaller companies and requires a higher return to accept that risk (Becker & Gray, 1999).

The reflection of non-systemic risk in the discount rate is particularly important for the evaluation of shares of privately owned companies (*Closely Held Companies*) because the owners of these shares do not diversify the portfolio like those who own publicly traded shares. Since the unsystematic part of the total risk will not be diversified to the same extent as in a portfolio of publicly traded stocks, at least some part of the unsystematic risk should be included in the estimation of the appropriate expected rate of return (Pratt & Grabowski, 2008). As measures of the size of share capital in determining the size premium, the following are used: market value of own capital, book value of ordinary shares, five-year average net profit. Furthermore, as measures of company size, the following are indispensable: market value of invested capital, total assets, five-year average EBITDA, net sales revenue and number of employees[1].

A size risk premium is generally applied to small businesses. According to studies conducted by Morningstar, excess returns increase proportionally as size decreases, and small-cap stocks have, on average, higher returns than large-cap stocks. The size risk premium according to the aforementioned analyzes is on average 2-6% (Morningstar, 2013). In order not to underestimate the risk of small companies in the CAPM, a premium for small companies can be added to the cost of own capital equal to the amount of the size premium; the yield of small stocks is so much higher compared to the stocks of large companies with the same betas. The size risk premium is an empirically derived correction to the CAPM. In this sense, the size risk premium in the extended CAPM is a complement to beta as a unique measure of risk, where it is necessary to identify the reasons for applying this premium. However, the recent trend question the treatment of size risk premium of small companies. According to the Morningstar, over the past 20 years (period 2004-2023), size risk premium was negative, suggesting the small companies had been achieving lower return compared to large companies. Small Research Index return of 8.9% underperforms the 10.1% return of the Large Research Index (difference in return is 1.2% per year) (Swedroe, 2024). This unusual issue related to size risk remains to be explained in next period.

A company-specific risk premium is used when the risk characteristics of a given company differ from those of competing companies in the industry. It includes specific factors that affect the competitive position in the industry or the level of risk perceived by investors. The application of this premium includes quantitative (comparison with leading or branch companies) and qualitative analysis (interviews and company

---

[1] These are the size factors that were used in the sector studies of companies from the database of the US Center for Research in Security Prices (CRSP) of the University of Chicago and the database of the Standard&Poor index (Standard&Poor Compustat database). The size studies present historical rates of return and equity risk premiums for 25 portfolios ranked by size according to eight specified size measures. Studies are updated annually, beginning in 1963, and demonstrate a relationship between historical returns and firm size (Grabowski, 2005 and King, 2003).

information). The level of the company-specific risk premium depends on several factors: size, industry risk, cash flow volatility, leverage and other specific risks. Companies can control the exposure to unsystematic risk through investments in HOV in certain economic branches. Measures of firm-specific risk that are correlated with historical rate of return are (Duff & Phelps, 2014):

- *Operating margin* (the lower the operating margin, the higher the risk);
- *Operating margin variation coefficient* (the higher the variation coefficient, the greater the risk);
- *Coefficient of variation of the return on the book value of the share* (the higher the coefficient, the higher the risk).

Like the size premium, the company-specific risk premium is most often associated with smaller companies, because as the size decreases, the company-specific risk, and thus the average risk, increases proportionally.

The industry risk premium is calculated using the information needed to calculate beta. The calculation of the total beta includes the weighting of the beta for the economic branch through beta companies that contribute to the given branch of activity with sales revenue. The weight for the company is obtained based on the share of the company's sales in the total branch sales.

For developing countries, the CAPM may include a country risk premium. Damodaran (2024) recommends a market risk premium which is the sum of the market risk premium from the mature capital market and the country risk premium. In the case of Bosnia and Herzegovina, market risk premium (ERP) in 2024 would amount to:

4.33% (average market equity risk premium in the US capital market) + 8.68% (country risk premium) = 13.01%.

The first way to determine the country risk premium is through the spread of the yield on the government bond in the given country and the yield on the US government bond. The national debt is ranked through rating agencies such as Moody's, S&P, etc. Bosnia and Herzegovina has a currency rating of B3 and a default spread of 6.44% is added to the market risk premium on the developed capital market based on that rating (Damodaran Database, 2025).

The second method uses stock market volatility as a base in the sense that higher standard deviation implies higher risk. The market risk premium is obtained as the sum of the market risk premium from the developed capital market and the relative standard deviation of a given developing country (say, Bosnia and Herzegovina).

The third way of calculating the country risk premium results in the highest country risk premium. The relative standard deviation of developing country X is calculated as the quotient of the standard deviation of the stock and the standard deviation of the developing country's domestic bond, and then multiplied by the default spread for the given country X.

A country risk premium is added to the cost of equity, but also to the cost of debt (over the default spread), using the economic parameters of each country. When using the country risk premium, the trap of double calculation of risk should be avoided. If, say, domestic bonds denominated in $ are used to determine the risk-free rate, they already include an implied premium. If country risk is also added, that risk will be counted twice, which is especially pronounced with betas adjusted downwards and cash flows adjusted upwards to take into account country risk (the so-called Haircutting) (Damodaran, 2012).

The country risk premium also uses lambda (λ) as a measure of country risk exposure. (Yim & Mitchell, 2005). Lambda is the quotient of the percentage of revenue that a given company achieves in the country and the percentage of revenue achieved by the average company on the market in the country (Damodaran, 2012):

$$\lambda \text{ (exposure to the country risk)} = \frac{\text{Precentage of revenues achieved in the country}_{\text{company X}}}{\text{Precentage of revenues achieved in the country}_{\text{average company in the country}}}$$

Another way of calculating lambda is from the ratio of return on shares and return on government bonds as a measure of country risk:

$$\text{Return}_{\text{stock}} = \text{a} + \lambda \text{Return}_{\text{government bond}}$$

The last lambda measure has a large standard error and implies the existence of a liquid government bond market, which is not the case with developing capital markets, so it is used less often. A lambda of 1 indicates average country risk exposure. Country risk exposure depends on:

- Sources of income (whether they come from placing products / services on the domestic market when the country's risk exposure is higher or on developed markets when this exposure is lower);
- Production facilities (e.g. mines have a significantly higher exposure to country risk);

- Risk management products (insurance against certain unpleasant circumstances or the use of derivatives reduces country risk).

Example 1. Calculating the cost of own capital with the country risk premium included. We determine the cost of capital for company X from Bosnia and Herzegovina. Let's assume that the calculated beta of this company is 1. The risk-free rate on the mature capital market, in this case the American one, is circa 4% (Damodaran database, 2025). To determine the total market risk premium for Company X, we include the country risk premium in the calculation by adding it to the amount of the mature equity market risk premium, which for the US is 4.33%. The country risk premium for Bosnia and Herzegovina is 8.68%. Assuming that country risk exposure is the same as total market risk exposure as measured by beta, it follows:

$$\begin{aligned}\text{Cost of equity} \\ &= \text{riskfree rate} + \beta \\ &\times (\text{Equity risk premium on the mature capital market} \\ &+ \text{country risk premium})\end{aligned}$$

$$\text{Cost of equity of company X in \$} = 4\% + 1\ \times (4.33\% + 8.68\%) = 17.01\%$$

The previous calculation of the cost of own capital is problematic for several reasons. Since the capital market will mature over time, the country risk will decrease, and thus the cost of own capital for company X. Also, the beta itself contains a certain level of country risk exposure. Furthermore, an export-oriented company will generate income abroad and be less exposed to country risk. In order to exclude the possibility of these errors, lambda - λ is introduced into the calculation of the cost of capital.

Company X is export-oriented and generates 70% of its sales revenue abroad. For an average company in Bosnia and Herzegovina, this rate is 14.9%, so lambda will be:

$$\lambda = \frac{\text{Precentage of revenues achieved in the country}_{\text{company X}}}{\text{Precentage of revenues achieved in the country}_{\text{ Bosnia and Herzegovina}}} = \frac{30\%}{85.1\%} = 0.35$$

Now the $ cost of equity for Company X will be significantly lower:

$$\begin{aligned}\text{Cost of Equity in \$} \\ &= \text{riskfree rate in US} \\ &+ \beta\ (\text{Equity risk premium on the mature capital market}) \\ &+ \lambda\ (\text{premija country risk premium})\end{aligned}$$

$$\text{Cost of Equity in \$} = 4\% + 1 \times 4.33\% + 0.35 \times 8.68\% = 11.37\%$$

The cost of own capital in $ can be translated into a real cost by taking into account the inflation ratio in the USA and Bosnia and Herzegovina. Then the cost of equity capital is:

$$\text{Cost of equity in BAM} = (1 + \text{cost of equity in \$}) \times \left(\frac{1 + \text{inflation rate}_{\text{BiH}}}{1 + \text{inflation rate}_{\text{US}}}\right) - 1$$
$$= (1 + 0.1137) \times \frac{1.033}{1.029} - 1 = 11.8\%$$

The difference in the cost of capital in $ and KM results from the difference in inflation rates in the two countries.

Another way is to immediately arrive at the cost of equity in local currency by taking the risk-free rate prevailing in that country (usually higher than in the US). For Bosnia and Herzegovina, the risk-free rate is the interest rate on government bonds, which is about 4.0%. Now the cost of equity capital will be:

$$\begin{aligned}\text{Cost of equity in BAM} \\ &= \text{riskfree rate in Bosnia in Herzegovina} \\ &* +\beta\ (\text{Equity risk premium on the mature capital market}) \\ &+ \lambda\ (\text{premija country risk premium}) \\ &= 4.1\% + 1 \times 4.33\% + 0.35 \times 8.68\% = 11.47\%\end{aligned}$$

*Risk free rate is rate on government bonds in Bosnia and Herzegovina

In this case the cost of capital is slightly higher than in the calculation in US dollars. The difference in the cost of own capital according to these two methods is of an accounting nature. The question arises whether to apply the country risk premium when calculating the cost of own capital? The first group of companies in this sense are companies that operate exclusively on the domestic market. It is obvious that these companies are not evaluated from the point of view of an international investor, and therefore do not imply the application of country risk. The other extreme is the possibility of complete diversification of developing country risk. If the company's marginal shareholder is globally diversified, there is no need to calculate country risk. If the portfolio were globally diversified, it would not be necessary to use the country risk premium (part of the country risk has become market or non-diversified risk). In all other cases, in the assessment of companies that are on the scale between these two extremes, it is necessary to include country risk in the calculation of the discount rate.

3. EMPIRICAL RESEARCH

In addition to consulting the relevant scientific literature, we used part of the empirical research conducted in 2015-2016 in Bosnia and Herzegovina, among members of the appraisal profession, to prove the views and support the conclusions. The data were collected using a questionnaire based on a random sample of 78 appraisers who have a certificate and license of an authorized appraiser. Statistical methods of data processing included descriptive statistics and statistical inference, i.e. chi-square test.

The analysis showed that the model for determining the discount rate used in the Bosnia and Herzegovina is significantly dominated by the build-up model, while the others are used significantly less, as can be seen in graph no. 2.

In the majority of cases, the respondents used the build-up model when determining the discount rate (89.7%), a simplified model, without including components such as the size risk premium (Rps) and the industry risk premium (RPi). Other company-specific factors are generally assessed.

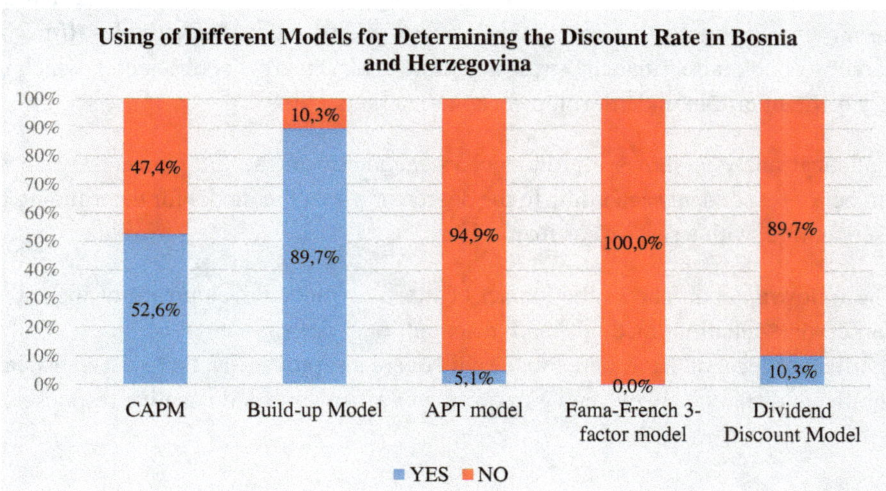

Chart 2: Models for Determining the Discount Rate in The Bosnia and Herzegovina

Source: Author´s calculation

The second most frequently used model is CAPM with 52.6%. The main reason for less use of CAPM is the problem of determining beta as a measure of systemic risk. Beta as a key component of the CAPM is difficult to determine in developing capital markets that do not have a stable trading history, rating agencies, or official publications of major houses that appraisers could use to calculate beta. On the other hand, in active capital markets, CAPM is mostly used to calculate the discount rate and is preferred by relevant authors in the field of valuation (Damodaran, 2012; Pratt & Grabowski, 2008; Pratt, 2009, etc.).

Other models are used in very few cases: APT in 5.1%, and the dividend discounting model in 10.3%. The APT model involves multiple regression and includes several risk factors: the risk of inflation, the so-called trust risk, time horizon risk and business cycle risk. APT is rarely applied even in developed capital markets because there is no general agreement on which variables in the equation would have the highest efficiency.

The dividend discounting model was used in a small number of assessments, because in the Bosnia and Herzegovina there is no regular practice of paying dividends and only a small number of companies continuously pay dividends. No one uses the Fama-French 3-factor model, which is not surprising given its complexity. This multiple linear regression model requires the inclusion of additional market variables (firm size, market-to-book ratio, financial stress and more critical market coefficients), which is a very difficult task in underdeveloped capital markets.

Statistical analysis shows a pronounced dependence in the difference between the number of respondents according to the degree of use of the model for determining the discount rate, with a risk of less than 0.1%.

The following chart shows the impact of inactivity/underdevelopment of the capital market on valuation methods and discount rate determination methods. With a significance level of 0.1%, here too the chi-square test proves that there is a statistically significant difference between the frequency of affirmative and negative responses.

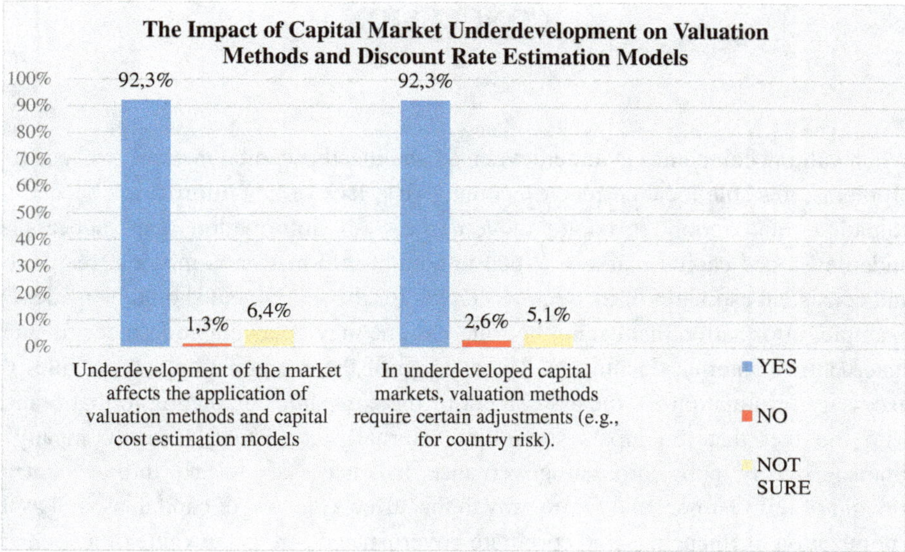

Chart 3: The Impact of Underdevelopment of The Capital Market on Valuation Methods and Discount Rate Calculation Models

Source: Author´s calculation

The inactivity or underdevelopment of the capital market affects the choice and application of assessment methods and models for determining the cost of capital, which is the opinion of 92.3% of respondents. Only 1.3% do not believe that the underdevelopment of the market affects the choice of methods and models, while 6.4% were undecided on this issue. In emerging capital markets, valuation methods require some adjustments. The vast majority of those surveyed, i.e. 92.3%, agree that in the conditions of an underdeveloped capital market, the methods should be adjusted, mainly for country risk. Only 2.6% disagreed.

The fact that appraisers during their work chose models for determining the cost of capital that are adapted to the business conditions of the company and the capital market in our country shows that the discount rate is considered an input whose change drastically affects the amount of the company's estimated value. This commitment to the formation of a relevant discount rate reflects the understanding of the importance of key parameters such as beta and country risk in the discount rate determination model.

CONCLUSION

When valuing companies in underdeveloped and inactive capital markets, we face four problems: unstable local currencies, country risk, lack of key information needed for valuation, and poor corporate governance. An information gap appears in underdeveloped capital markets. When important information is missing, reasonable and consistent estimates of the required inputs for the assessment should be made. For example, information that cannot be found in one may be available in other financial statements or internal documents. The average of the economic branch provides the necessary information for the assessment of the companies belonging to that branch, with the fact that the inputs should be internally consistent. If the company is characterized by poor corporate governance, it is necessary to take into account the amount of reinvestment and future growth that affects the cost of capital, as well as the optimization of financing. Bad corporate governance destroys the value of a company and this should be borne in mind if changes in managers are rare and slow.

A major problem that occurs with companies in underdeveloped capital markets is the double or incorrect calculation of country risk. By using foreign currency, country risk is sometimes omitted from the assessment, which leads to an overestimation of the company's value. Expected cash flows, although they include the possibility of bad business, are often not adjusted to reflect country risk. Appraisers may assume that beta includes all country risk, however, this is not very likely because firms in inactive and underdeveloped capital markets are generally smaller in size. The other extreme is too much concern about country risk when it is built into every dimension of risk: higher risk-free rates, higher equity risk premiums, and reduced expected cash flows leading to double or triple country risk accounting.

Risk parameters, beta and default spread for underdeveloped/inactive capital markets are influenced by the illiquidity and volatility of capital markets and the absence of bond ratings for most companies. Data and comparable companies from developed capital markets can be used to determine beta (Bottom-up method), especially if the company has securities listed on a foreign, developed capital market. The default range is reached through the so-called synthetic rating using the interest coverage ratio.

There are two important questions: *how to best estimate the risk premium for a specific market and the exposure of a given company to country risk*. The first group of companies in this sense are companies that operate exclusively on the domestic market. It is obvious that these companies are not evaluated from the point of view of an international investor, and therefore do not imply the application of country risk. The other extreme, when there will be no premium for country risk, is in the case of the possibility of complete diversification of country risk (which is unlikely in practice, except for large multinational corporations). In all other cases, in the assessment of companies that are on the scale between these two extremes, it is necessary to include country risk in the calculation of the discount rate. Specifically, the default spread for domestic government bonds, the volatility of emerging versus developed capital markets and a composite measure that raises the default spread for a bond (over relative stock market volatility) are used to determine the country risk premium.

The inclusion of country risk in the discount rate can be done as part of the beta calculation or as part of the risk premium calculation. As exposure to country risk is not the same for all companies, beta as an established risk parameter can be used to capture country risk. Assuming that exposure to country risk is the same as exposure to total market risk as measured by beta, stocks with a beta greater than 1 will be more exposed to country risk. In this way, it is simple to determine the country risk premium, but beta, as already said, although it reflects macroeconomic risk is not the best measure of country risk. Another way of including country risk in the discount rate is through the country risk premium and using lambda as a measure of the international openness of the company. By including lambda in the calculation of the risk premium, it is possible for each company to measure the exposure to country risk separately from the exposure to other market risks. Therefore, the system framework for assessing the value of companies in developing markets includes the choice of currency for evaluation, measurement of country risk and exposure of a given company to country risk via beta or lambda, search for missing information in alternative sources and assessment of cash flows that reflect the quality of management.

REFERENCES

Becker, B., & Gray, I. (1999). Does a Small Firm Effect Exist When Using the CAPM? Not Since 1980 and When Using Geometric Means of Historical Returns. *Business Valuation Review, 18(3)*, 104–111.

Bhattacharya, S. N., & Bhattacharya, M. (2013). Long Memory in Return Structures From Developed Markets. *Cuadernos de Gestión*, *13*(2), 127-143.

Brealey, R., Myers, S., & Marcus, A. (2011). *Fundamentals of Corporate Finance*. McGraw Hill.

Cai, C. X., Clacher, I., & Keasey, K. (2013). Consequences of the Capital Asset Pricing Model (CAPM) - a Critical and Broad Perspective. *Abacus*, Accounting Foundation, University of Syndey, *49*, 51-61. https://doi.org/10.1111/abac.2013.49.issue-s1

Copeland, T., Koller T., & Murrin, J. (2000). *Valuation: Measuring and Managing the Value of Companies*. John Wiley and Sons.

Damodaran, A. (2012). *Investment Valuation*: *Tools and Techniques for Determining the Value of Any Asset.* 3rd Ed. John Wiley and Sons.

Damodaran, A. (2025) *Database: Country Default Spreads and Risk Premiums*. https://pages.stern.nyu.edu/~adamodar/New_Home_Page/datafile/ctryprem.html

Duff & Phelps. (2014). *2014 Valuation Handbook*. Duff & Phelps. http://www.duffandphelps.com/SiteCollectionDocuments/Services/Valuation/2014%20Valuation%20Handbook%20Updates%20Clarifications.pdf.

Fama, E. F., & French, K. R. (2002). The Equity Premium. *Journal of Finance*, *57*(2), 637–659.

Grabowski, R. (2005). Equity Risk Premium: What Is the Current Evidence? In Pratt, S. *Business Valuation Update*. November 2005, 1–7.

King, D. (2003). Do Data Biases Cause the Small Stock Premium? *Business Valuation Review, June* 2003, 55–61.

Koller, T., Goedhart, M., & Wessels, D. (2010). *Valuation: Measuring and Managing the Value of Companies.* John Wiley and Sons.

Meitner M., & Streitferdt, F. G. (2014). DCF-Valuations of Companies in Crisis: Distress-Related Leverage, Identification of Risk Positions, Discounting Techniques, and "Beta Flips". *Journal of Business Valuation and Economic Loss Analysis, 9*(1), 145-174. https://doi.org/10.1515/jbvela-2013-0019

Mikerević, D. (2009). *Principi i praksa procjene vrijednosti preduzeća.* Finrar Banja Luka.

Morningstar. (2013). *SBBI Valuation Edition 2013 Yearbook.* Morningstar. http://corporate.morningstar.com/ib/asp/detail.aspx?xmlfile=1431.xml.

Pereiro, L. E. (2006). The Practice of Investment Valuation in Emerging Markets: Evidence from Argentina. *Journal of Multinational Financial Management, 16*(2), 160-183. https://doi.org/10.1016/j.mulfin.2005.06.001

Pratt, S. (2008). *Valuing a Business: The Analysis and Appraisal of Closely Held Companies.* Mc Graw Hill.

Pratt, S. & Grabowski, R. J. (2008). *Cost of Capital: Estimation and Applications. 3rd Ed.* John Wiley and Sons.

Salomons, R., & Grootveld, H. (2003). The Equity Risk Premium: Emerging vs Developed Markets. *Emerging Markets Review. Elsevier, 4*(2), 121-144. https://doi.org/10.1016/S1566-0141(03)00024-4

Statista. (2024). *Average market risk premium in the United States from 2011 to 2024.* https://www.statista.com/statistics/664840/average-market-risk-premium-usa/

Swedroe, L. (2024). *What Happened to the Size Premium?* https://www.morningstar.com/alternative-investments/what-happened-size-premium

Yim, J., & Mitchell, H. (2005). Comparison of Country Risk Models: Hybrid Neural Networks, Logit Models, Discriminant Analysis and Cluster Techniques. *Expert Systems with Applications, 28*(1), 137-148. https://doi.org/10.1016/j.eswa.2004.08.005

II [*]THE EFFECT OF MARKET LIQUIDITY ON THE COMPANY VALUE

Abstract

Market liquidity as an important factor of making investment decisions at the capital market, provides security for the investors and reduces the risk of not being able to close their positions without significant loss of financial assets. Less liquid market brings higher yields due to greater price volatility, but withdraws a greater risk. Liquidity is considered a primary factor in the development of capital markets. Generally, market liquidity is based on the existence of a great number of buyers and sellers at any time, the possibility of carrying out subsequent transactions at the same price as the previous one and the market ability to absorb buying and selling the larger quantities of the securities without significantly affecting the price.

In theory, there are strong evidences suggesting market liquidity has a positive impact on performance, and thus on the company value. Companies with shares listed on liquid markets and generally with more liquid shares, generate higher returns on assets and have more equity in the capital structure. One of the ways to measure the market liquidity is over the impact of the amount of traded stocks on the market price. Researches made in emerging markets showed that there was an 80% correlation between the spread of purchasing and selling prices and market liquidity. With the reduction of difficulties in trading related to prices, volume and market capitalization, the level of market liquidity increases. As the cash flow and control rights of the company are essentially determined by company shares, the marketability of shares will undoubtedly play a decisive role in corporate governance, assessing the value and performances of the company.

The purpose of this paper is to show that that market liquidity has a positive impact on the performance and operating profitability of the companies, and thereby on the value of the companies. Empirical analysis proved that companies with more liquid shares, traded on more regular basis, had higher operating income which was increasing business value. Another basis for the growing performance of the companies with liquid shares is by increasing the incentive effects of managerial contract founded on

---

[*] *Originally published in 2015 in the Proceedings of the REDETE 2015 Conference of Faculty of Economics University of Banja Luka, Graz, pp. 832–843.*

performance on more liquid markets. Information feedback that managers and other shareholders are getting over the market price of shares is responsible for the better performance of companies whose shares are quoted on the more liquid capital markets.

Keywords: *market liquidity, performances, company value, market price, shares*

INTRODUCTION

Market liquidity as an important factor of making investment decisions at the capital market, provides security for the investors and reduces the risk of not being able to close their positions without significant loss of financial assets. Considering the complexity of the liquidity term, there is more than one definition of liquidity. Generally, liquid market can be described as one where participants can quickly accomplish large transactions with no significant impact on the price. How can the liquidity on the capital market be measured?

One way to measure market liquidity is over the impact of the quantity of shares which were traded on the market price, as Pástor and Stambaug (2003) demonstrated in their study. There is a correlation between market liquidity and shares yields (Amihud & Mendelson, 1986). Liquidity variations are correlated with monetary policy and have an effect on shares and bonds (Chordia, Sarkar & Subrahmanyam, 2005). The liquidity of capital markets is defined by four aspects (von Wyss, 2004):

- *Trading time* (the ability to perform the transactions immediately and at the prevailing price);
- *Density / compaction* (capability of simultaneous purchase and sale at approximately equal price);
- *Depth* (possibility of buying or selling certain assets without affecting the price);
- *Elasticity / resistance* (the ability of simultaneous purchase or sale without a significan influence on the price, taking into account not only the volume but also the elasticity of supply and demand).

These dimensions of liquidity can be observed at five different levels of liquidity:

- Trading possibility;
- Possibility of buying and selling sertain amount of securities with an impact on the price;
- Possibility of buying and selling sertain amount of securities without affecting the price;
- Possibility of simultaneous buying and selling of securities at approximately equal price;
- Possibility of immediate trading.

Liquidity is considered a primary factor in the development of capital markets. Companies with shares listed on liquid markets and generally with more liquid shares, generate higher returns on assets and have more equity in the capital structure. Researches done in the emerging markets showed that there is a correlation of 80 percent between the range of bid and offer prices and market liquidity (Levy Yeyati, Schmukler & Van Horen, 2007. With decrease in trading difficulties related to prices, volume and market capitalization, the level of market liquidity increases (Lesmond, 2005, p. 37). Thus, a liquid market is the one where participants can quickly accomplish large transactions with no significant impact on the price.

The paper focuses on the hypothesis that market liquidity has a positive impact on the performance and operating profitability of the companies, and thereby on the value of the companies. In order to confirm this conclusion, the measures of market liquidity have been analysed, and the overview of previous research and studies of this subject has been given. Then we have specified the methodology for empirical analysis we used in our work, presented and discussed research results and provided appropriate attitudes and conclusions of researh topic.

1. MEASURES OF MARKET LIQUIDITY

Liquidity measures can be classified into two cathegories: one-dimensional and multidimensional, depending on the number of variables covered. One-dimensional liquidity measures are divided into four groups (Benić & Franić, 2008):

1) Measures for analysing the size of the company.

The market capitalization expresses the company value as the multiplicator of the number of issued shares (Si) and their market price (Pi): $Mcap_i = Si \times Pi$. Number of shares actually available on the market can be used for more precise liquidity measurement (Free Float).

2) Measures that represent the volume (quantity of shares) per time unit.

a) The *volume* represents the number of shares traded in a certain period of time - high volume withdraws higher market liquidity.

b) *Turnover* is the multiplicator of price (pi) and the quantity of shares in the transaction (qi) in a certain time interval (t):

$$Tn = \sum_{i=1}^{Nt} p_i \times q_i;$$

c) Turnover is a more significant measure of volume because it allows comparison of more different shares. When turnover is analyzed together with a market capitalization, the result is *trade turnover* that determines how many times securities have changed owners:

Trade turnover = Tn / Mcap.

d) *Indicator of average daily change in value of the market index* shows volatility of the market. The lower value of this indicator (less price change) means higher liquidity.

e) *The ratio of the average daily change of the index and the trade turnover* shows the impact of turnover and market capitalization on the volatility of prices. (Sarr & Lybek, 2002). The lower ratio is, liquidity and market efficiency is higher. If this indicator is low, the market depth is not satisfactory, respectively high-value transactions affect the price because there are not enough large and numerous orders with low price range.

3) *Measures of liquidity associated with time* - show frequency of market transactions.

High frequency of transaction execution and shorter time between transactions suggest that the market is liquid. The *number of orders* in a certain time period is also a measure of liquidity belonging this group of measures, which is important in comparing the situation in several capital markets.

4) *Measures associated with the spread (the difference between bid and selling price)* –show amount of costs associated with trading.

Absolute or quoted spread is the difference between the highest bid and the lowest selling price. This spread is always positive under the condition the trading is regular. The lower limit of the spread is minimal money unit permitted on the capital market. Market liquidity is higher as the measures of spread are lower.

Multi-dimensional liquidity measures are the following (Benić & Franić, 2008):

1) *Amivest liquidity ratio* relates securities trading volume in certain period with the percentage of price change in absolute terms:

$$\mathrm{LR1}_t = \frac{\mathrm{Tn}_t}{\mathrm{Ir_tI}} = \frac{\sum_{i=1}^{N} p_i \times q_i}{\mathrm{Ir_tI}}$$

Meaning: $\mathrm{LR1}_t$ - liquidity ratio in time, r_t - percentage of price change (yield), expressed in absolute terms, Tn – trade, N- number of transactions in the time period t, p_i – price, q_i - quantity of securities in the transaction.

Higher ratio means that the market is possible to absorb a larger price changes viz. market is more liquid.

2) *Amihud illiquidity measure* shows the percentage of price change in absolute terms and the trading volume (Amihud 2002, according Benić & Franić, 2008):

$$ILLIQ_t = \frac{1}{LR1_t} = \frac{\mathrm{Ir_tI}}{\mathrm{Tn}}$$

This indicator analyzes several measures of liquidity, respectively price change, trading volume and the impact of trading volume on the price. It shows the influence of one KM (or dollar) on the percentage of daily price change in the market. A lower value of measure indicates a higher market liquidity, and vice versa.

In analysing the liquidity of certain market it is necessary to apply more measures in order to gain the right information of existence of liquidity and the degree of market illiquidity. Companies with more liquid shares traded on more regular basis have higher operating income, which is ultimately increasing company value. Furthermore, performances of the companies with liquid shares are growing by increasing the incentive effects of managerial contract founded on performance on more liquid markets.

2. THE OVERVIEW OF PREVIOUS RESEARCH ON MARKET LIQUIDITY

The effect of liquidity on the performances of the company is in the focus of causal theories based on agency costs. One of the most important representatives of these theories is Maug (2002), who believes that liquid markets support effective corporate governance. Market liquidity can not be considered separately from trading with private information on the capital markets nor from monitoring of companies by large investors in order to realize capital gains on shares. Liquid capital markets contribute to resolving the lack of information. In less liquid market large investors will choose a smaller stake to diversify risk. According to Edmans (2009), the majority shareholders in the market behave as informed participants, not as control subjects and their added value of majority shareholders should depend on liquidity. Reducing market liquidity and increasing the share of majority shareholders control imply that the stakes of large shareholders become less liquid. Although these two actions reduce the liquidity of large blocks of shares, they have the opposite effect on the monitoring - reducing market liquidity decreases monitoring. (Maug, 2002, p. 68). The growth of the required control stake forces majority shareholders to accumulate a larger block of shares in order to maintain control which means they need to take a higher level of monitoring in the future.

The expected profit increase of monitored companies is always included in the share price. The only source of profit from the monitoring for large investors arises from the uncertainty of the final payment. Profit comes from an increase in volatility, not from change in the refund amount. If capital markets are less liquid, large shareholders will be less engaged around monitoring. In order to avoid the obligation for monitoring, they will diversify their portfolio that is they will possess smaller stakes in several companies. Liquid share market leads to greater monitoring because it allows the investor to cover the costs of monitoring through trading based on relevant information. When a large shareholder can choose between monitoring and acquisition as various forms of intervention in companies that operate with loss, they will prefer: less expensive method if the market is not liquid and more effective method if the capital market is liquid.

Liquid markets increase the possibility of successful corporate restructuring in two ways. As the first, liquid markets allow shareholders to realize gains from monitoring through informed trading, and secondly, they ensure application of the restructuring method because of its efficiency, not lower price (Maug, 2002). Rent which large shareholders draw from the company monitoring can be reduced if larger packages of voting rights are required, forcing large shareholders to concentrate their stakes (large stakes are therefore less liquid). Higher demands for majority control increase initial stakes, reduce rents and enhance the tendency to monitoring.

In theory there are strong evidences suggesting that market liquidity affects positively the performance and thus the value of the company. Since the shares are determinant which is crucial for determining cash flow and control rights, marketability of shares will undoubtedly have a decisive role in corporate governance, value appraissal and performancs of the company. Liquid markets allow purchase of a large or a control block of shares, reduce opportunism of managers, promote a more efficient system of managers remuneration and stimulate trade between informed investors thereby improving investment decisions through more informative share prices (Khanna & Sonti, 2004).

Numerous papers have been supporting the claim that market liquidity has effect on the performances of the company. Highly liquid shares used to calculate the ratios such as market-to-book ratio show better performance. Market-to-book ratio is a very good starting indicator in calculating different measures of liquidity. Companies with shares quoted on liquid capital markets and generally with more liquid shares, achieve higher returns on assets and have more equity in the capital structure. On the other hand, the price-operative earnings ratio is similar for liquid and for illiquid shares. These conclusions are valid in determining controlling stake for the industrial branch, the level of shareholder rights, risk and the moment when return to shares is achieved (Fang, Noe & Tice, 2009, p. 151). Furthermore, exogenous shocks and changes in the environment in terms of liquidity indicate that major changes in the shares liquidity lead to major changes in the performances of the company.

Subrahmanyam and Titman (2001) in their study of the relationship between share prices and company's cash flow have showed that the positive effects of a liquid market on the performances of companies is greater for liquid shares with high business uncertainty (high volatility of operating income and intense investment in research and development). Liquid markets allow informed investors to expose private information and profit from them. With the higher inflow of such information, the results of greater liquidity are increasing gains from the use of compensation based on shares. However, liquidity does not increase or diminish the effects of performances on shareholder rights. The market liquidity positive effect on performances comes from improving the incentive effects of the compensation in shares and improving investment decisions of corporate insiders.

In an extensive study Fang, Noe and Tice (2009) have analyzed the correlation between market liquidity and the performance of companies, measured by Tobin's Q indicator. They used the indicator of the effective range based on daily TAQ[2] data, which is considered to be one of the best shares liquidity representative. To check indicators power, they used three alternative measures of liquidity: adjusted measure of illiquidity (Amihud, 2002), measure of liquidity based on a percentage of zero daily returns (Lesmond, Ogden and Trzcinka, 1999) and the relative quota range on TAQ data basis..

The indicators on Tobin's Q basis has been used as a measure of companies' performances. Tobin's Q is used in a number of similar studies and represents the ratio of the company's market value and the costs of replacing its assets. Indicator Q in Fang, Noe and Tice (2009) expresses the quotient of the assets market value and assets book value of the company at the end of the fiscal year. In addition, there have been calculated earnings-to-price ratio as the value of the operating income after depreciation divided by the market value of common shares and financial leverage ratio as a proportion of equity in the market value of the company's assets. All measures have revealed similar results, proving that market liquidity positively affects the performances and value of the company.

[2] TAQ (The Trade and Quote) is a database that contains the daily trading and quotas of all securities listed on the New York Stock Exchange, American Stock Exchange, the NASDAQ national system of trading and securities of relatively small market capitalization (SmallCap issues). TAQ provides information about all securities quoted on the New York Stock Exchange since 1993.

3. METHODOLOGICAL FRAMEWORK FOR EMPIRICAL ANALYSIS

Illiquidity of the capital market and its impact on the performance and operating profitability of the companies, and thereby on the value of the companies are subject for a number of foreign studies, as well as few domestic analyses. Liquid markets allow informed investors to expose private information and profit from them. Results of other studies (Maug, 2002; Subrahmanyam & Titman, 2001; Khanna & Sonti, 2004; Fang, Noe & Tice, 2009) compared with ours, confirmed our hypothesis. Relevant information found on liquid capital market such as New York Stock Exchange prove that companies with more liquid shares have more success in corporate governance and higher operative business result. The main aim of this research is to confirm that liquidity of market and the marketability of shares (having in mind that cash flow and control rights are determined by shares) will be decisive factor in corporate governance, assessing the value and performances of the company.

We used information obtained by interviewing 78 certified appraisers in period 2015-2016 in Bosnia and Herzegovina, who owned the license for evaluation. Most of the questions are of closed type: direct questions, questions with multiple choices and intensity questions. Respondents highlighted the characteristics of market illiquidity, which they believed existing in the Bosnia and Herzegovina. Furthmore, respondents gave their opinion about the characteristics and intensity of market illiquidity and how that affected their choice of methods and approaches they used performing their appraisal work. They answered the question about the coorelation between the market liquidity and performance of the companies they evaluated. Also, respondents declare on effect of managerial contract on companies' performance on capital market in Bosnia and Herzegovina.

The survey was limited to the examination of illiquidity of capital market in the Bosnia and Herzegovina. We also used data from the Banja Luka and Sarajevo Stock Exchange, Republic of Srpska Institute of Statistics, as well as data from New York Stock Exchange, International Monetary Fund, World Bank and studies of other relevant instututions and authors.

4. RESULTS OF ANALYSIS AND DISCUSION

Foremost, the research results show a high degree of agreement of respondents with the statement that the capital market in Bosnia and Herzegovina is illiquide. 94% of total number of respondents believe that the capital market is not liquid, while 6% of the respondents did not answer the question. Of those interviewed, none has said that the capital market in the country is liquid.

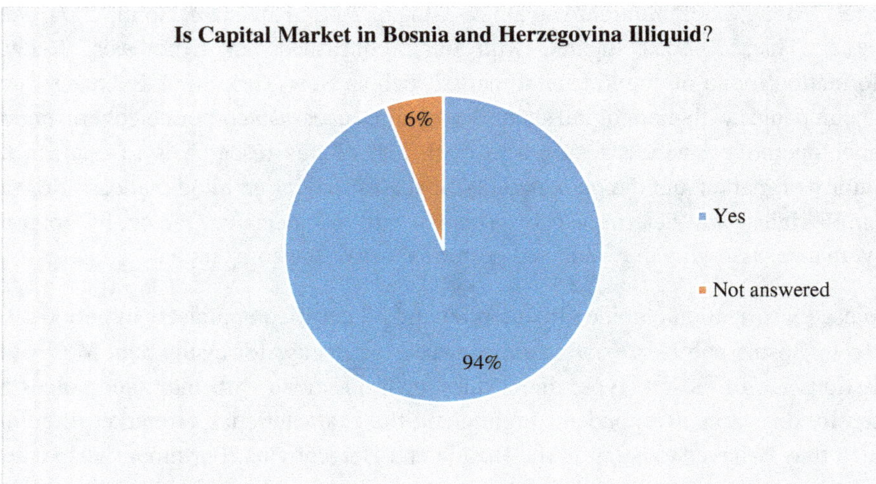

Chart 1: Capital Market Iliquidity in Bosnia and Herzegovina

Source: Author's survey

Respondents have agreed that all features of illiquid capital are characteristic for capital market in Bosnia and Herzegovina, only the degrees of manifestation of certain features are different.

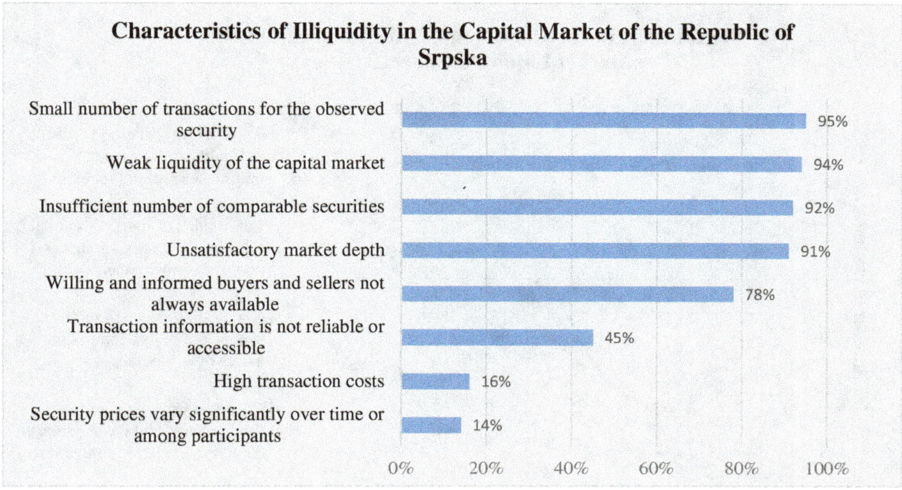

Chart 2: Characteristics of Illiquidity in Bosnia and Herzegovina Capital Market

Source: Author's survey

Results indicate that 95% of respondents believe that there are small number of transactions for observed security or securities with similar characteristics on our capital market. Also, poor market liquidity and insufficient depth of the capital market (number and financial potential of buyers and sellers) are observed by 94% and 91% of surveyed appraisers, respectively. Likewise, the interviewees have found that the insufficient number of similar securities that are comparable with the observed one is significant problem in our capital market (92%). Somewhat smaller number of respondents are convinced that they can find a willing and informed buyers and sellers at any time (78%).

However, less than half of the respondents, that is 45%, think that information about the transactions are not reliable and available. The least marked characteristic of illiquid capital market are the high transaction costs (16%) and a significant variation of securities prices over time or between market participants (14%).

Obviously, the capital market in the Bosnia and Herzegovina is characterized as illiquid with all features of illiquidity at lower or higher extent.

The importance and the level of significance of market liquidity that respondents assigned to specific statements related to value and performance of companies are presented on following graph.

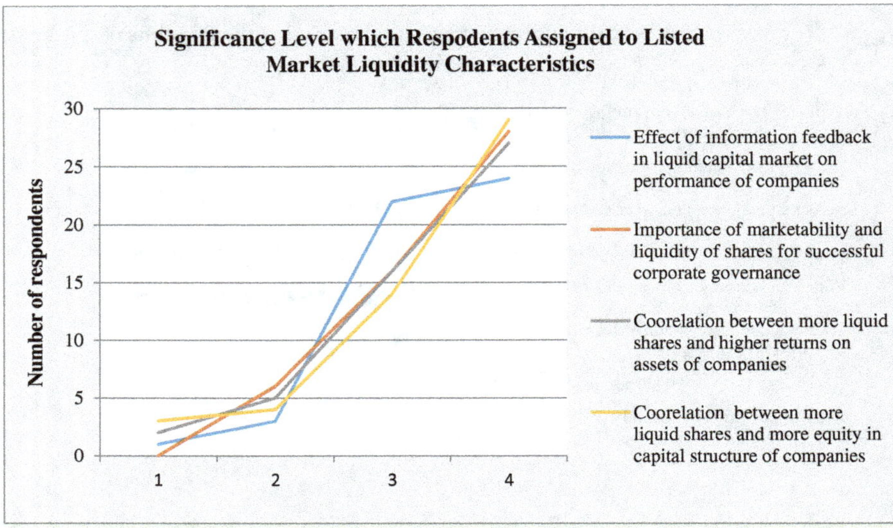

Chart 3: Significance of Capital Market Liquidity for Performance, Return on Assets and Capital Structure of Companies

Source: Author's survey

Examinees marked theses related to market liquidity as not important (1), less important (2), medium important (3) and very important (4). Examined theses are:

3. Effect of information feedback in liquid capital market on performance of companies;
4. Importance of marketability and liquidity of shares for succesfull corporate governance;
5. Coorelation between more liquid shares and higher return on asset of companies;
6. Coorelation between more liquid shares and higher level of equity in capital structure of companies.

Respondents have decided if four listed theses are less or more important. Effect of information feedback in liquid capital market on performance of companies is marked as not important by 2% and less important by 6% of examinees. Cumulatively, majority of examinees beleive that information are of medium importance (44%) or of high importance (48%) for result and performance of companies.

The importance of marketability and liquidity of shares for succesfull corporate governance is low for 12% of respondents, but medium for 32% and high for 56% of respondents, respectively. Obviously, majority of respondents think that marketability and liquidity of shares are of the highest importance for efficient menagement business.

The coorelation between more liquid shares and higher return on asset of companies is very strong according to 54% of respondents and medium strong for 32% of them. 10% of respondents marked this coorelation as less strong and only 4% of respondents see mentioned coorelation as weak.

The coorelation between more liquid shares and highere level of equity in capital structure of companies is determined as medium strong by 28% of respondents and as very strong by 58% of them. Similar like in previos thesis, 6% and 8% of examinees think that this coorelation is weak and less strong, respectively.

Conclusion following from all listed results is that in liquid capital market companies have higher returns, more equity in capital structure, better performance as well as more successful menagement, due to increasing incentive effects of managerial contracts. Thus, liquid capital market leads to higher value of companies listed on that market. More equity in capital structure of companies listed on liquid markets is explained by more effective share issues and continuous and regular shares trading.

Table 1: Some of precedences of liquid capital market

Liquid market enables:	Percentage of respondents who agreed with statement
Facilitating purchase of control or large block of shares	76%
Decreasing opportunism of menagers	67%
More efficient system of rewarding menagers	69%
Stimulation of trading between informed market participants / investors	89%
Improving investment decisions and corporate governance	72%

Source: Author's survey

Previous table presents results from analysis of some effects of liquid markets. 76% of examinees consider that liquid market enables easier purchase of control or large blocks of shares. Decreasing opportunism of menagers and more efficient system of rewarding menagers are assigned as characteristics of liquid markets by 67% and 69% of respondents, respectively. Stimulation of trading between informed market participants/investors is enabled by liquid market according to 89% of examinees. Finally, liquid market enables improving investment decisions and corporate governance as it is concluded by 72% of respondents. This is also presented on the graph.

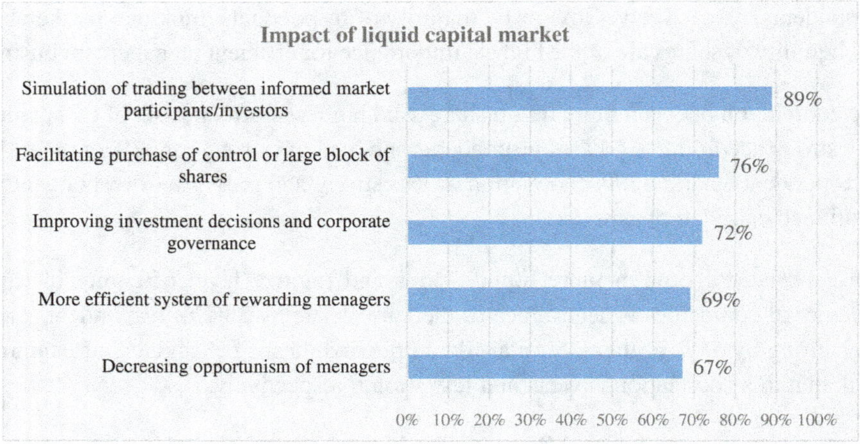

Chart 4: Impact of Liquid Capital Market

Source: Author's survey

The great majority of respondents agreed that liquid capital markets has positive impact on many aspects of operating business. On the other hand, in Bosnia and Herzegovina, capital market is illiquid which means that companies are faced with lower performances, more difficulties in gathering equity capital and achiving positive business results. The analysis showed that due to lack of liquidity in capital market in Bosnia and Herzegovina, appraisals are limited in using some of the methods of appraisal, especially methods of market approach. When market is illiquid, market value as the most reliable concept of value does not correspond conditions of appraisal, so other concepts such as fair value or special value have to be used. This means that illiquide capital market significantly restricts possibility of using certain appraisal approaches and concepts which results in less reliable and representative value of companies. The causal coorelation between less relevant company value achieved in appraisals and lower performanse on iliquid market is found to be existing in capital market of Bosnia and Herzegovina.

CONCLUSION

The market liquidity is based on the existence of a large number of buyers and sellers at any moment, ability to perform the following transaction at the same price as the previous one and the market capacity to absorb buying and selling larger amounts of securities without significantly affecting the price. The liquidity of capital markets is defined by four aspects: trading time, density/compaction, depth and elasticity/resistance. Liquidity measures are classified into two cathegories: one-dimensional and multidimensional. One-dimensional measures include: measures for analysing the size of the company, measures that represent the volume (quantity of shares) per time unit, measures associated with the spread and measures of liquidity associated with time. Multidimensional measures is consisting of Amivest liquidity ratio and Amihud illiquidity measure.

Results of the other authors' studies showed that the market liquidity positively affect the performance and operating profitability of the company. Causes of these results also have been examined and there has been provided empirical support for models of share price as well as for the view that liquidity improves the value of management compensation linked to the results achievement. In order to identify the causal effects of market liquidity on performance, the effect of exogenous shocks on liquidity has been tested theoretically. Increasing liquidity in the months of exogenous shocks enhance performance by boosting operating income. Liquid share market leads to greater monitoring because it allows the investor to cover the costs of monitoring through trading based on relevant information. Liquid markets increase the possibility of successful corporate restructuring by allowing shareholders to realize gains from monitoring through informed trading and by ensuring application of the restructuring method based on efficiency, not lower price. Market liquidity can not be considered separately from trading with private information on the capital markets nor from monitoring of companies by large investors in order to realize capital gains on shares.

Empirical analysis conducted in Bosnia and Herzegovina envince that all features of illiquid capital are characteristic for capital market in Bosnia and Herzegovina, only the manifestation degrees of certain features are different. Significance of capital market liquidity for performance, return on assets and capital structure of companies was also demonstrated. Finding following from all listed results is that in liquid capital market companies have higher returns, more equity in capital structure, better performance as well as more successful menagement, due to increasing incentive effects of managerial contracts. Information feedback over the shares market price which are getting managers and other stakeholders is responsible for the better performance of companies whose shares are quoted on the more liquid capital markets. Thus, liquid capital market leads to higher value of companies listed on that market.

More equity in capital structure of companies listed on liquid markets is explained by more effective share issues and continuous and regular shares trading. This means that illiquide capital market significantly restricts possibility of using certain appraisal approaches and concepts which results in less reliable and representative value of companies. The causal coorelation between less relevant company value achieved in appraisals and lower performanse on iliquid market is found to be existing in capital market of Bosnia and Herzegovina. We conclude that the market liquidity improves the performance of the company over the higher operating income, which finally increases the value of the company.

REFERENCES

Amihud, Y. (2002). Illiquidity and stock returns: cross-section and time-series effects. *Journal of Financial Markets, 5*(1), 31-56. https://doi.org/10.1016/S1386-4181(01)00024-6

Amihud, Y., & Mendelson, H. (1986). Asset pricing and the bid-ask spread. *Journal of Financial Economics, 17*(2), 223-249. https://doi.org/10.1016/0304-405X(86)90065-6

Banja Luka Stock Exchange. (n.d.). www.blberza.com

Benić, V., & Franić, I. (2008). Komparativna analiza likvidnosti tržište kapitala Hrvatske i zemalja regije. *Financijska teorija i praksa, 32*(4), 481-502.

Chordia, T., Sarkar, A., & Subrahmanyam, A. (2005). An Empirical Analysis of Stock and Bond Market Liquidity. *Review of Financial Studies, 18*(1), 85-129.

Edmans, A. (2009). Block holder trading, market efficiency and managerial myopia. *Journal of finance, 64*(6), 2481-2513. https://doi.org/10.1111/j.1540-6261.2009.01508.x

Fang, V. W., Noe, T. H., & Tice, S. (2009). Stock market liquidity and firm value. *Journal of Financial Economics, 94*(1), 150-169.

International Monetary Fund. (n.d.). www.imf.org

Khanna, N., & Sonti, R. (2004). Value creating stock manipulation: feedback effect of stock prices on firm value. *Journal of Financial Markets, 7*(3), 237-270.

Lesmond, D. A. (2005). Liquidity of Emerging Markets. *Journal of Financial Economics, 77*(2), 411-452. https://doi.org/10.1016/j.jfineco.2004.01.005

Lesmond, D. A., Ogden, J., & Trzcinka, C. (1999). A new estimate of transaction costs. *Review of Financial Studies, 12*(5), 1113-1141.

Levy Yeyati, E., Schmukler, S., & Van Horen, N. (2007). *Emerging Market Liquidity and Crises.* Policy Research, Working Paper, 4445. The World Bank. http://wwwwds.worldbank.org/external/default/WDSContentServer/WDSP/IB/2007/12/13/000158349_20071213152426/Rendered/PDF/wps4445.pdf

Maug, E. (2002). Large shareholders as monitors: Is there a trade-off between liquidity and control? *Journal of Finance*, *53*(1), 65-98. https://doi.org/10.1111/0022-1082.35053

New York Stock Exchange. (n.d.). www.nyse.com

Pástor, L., & Stambaugh, R. (2003). Liquidity risk and expected stock returns. *Journal of Political Economy*, *111*(3), 642-685. http://dx.doi.org/10.1086/374184

Republic of Srpska Institute of Statistics. (n.d.). www.rzs.rs.ba

Sarr, A., & Lybek, T. (2002). Measuring Liquidity in Financial Markets. *IMF Working Paper WP/02/232*. http://www.imf.org/external/pubs/ft/wp/2002/wp02232.pdf

Subrahmanyam, A., & Titman, S. (2001). Feedback from stock prices to cash flows. *Journal of finance*, *56*(6), 2389-2413. https://doi.org/10.1111/0022-1082.00409

Von Wyss, R. (2004). *Measuring and Predicting Liquidity in the Stock Market*. [Doctoral dissertation, University of St. Gallen]. St. Gallen

World Bank. (n.d.). www.worldbank.org

III *VALUATION OF COMPANIES IN TERMS OF AN INACTIVE CAPITAL MARKET

Abstract

Determining the value of a company in an inactive capital market is far from simple. It is evident that in such markets, the process of obtaining inputs for valuation is significantly more complex, and the determined value itself is less reliable due to factors such as lack of transparency, limited availability of information, and other inherent risks. In the valuation of companies under conditions of an inactive capital market, it is essential to analyze the relevance of transaction prices compared to other fair value indicators. The significance of a transaction depends on factors such as transaction volume, the proximity of the transaction date to the valuation date, and the comparability of the transaction with the asset or liability being valued. This paper is based on two hypotheses. The first is that the capital market in the Bosnia and Herzegovina is inactive and underdeveloped. The second hypothesis is that an inactive capital market significantly limits and determines the applicability of valuation approaches and methods, the cost of capital, as well as value concepts. Accordingly, in inactive capital markets, a prerequisite for a relevant company valuation is a prior analysis of transaction price significance and the characteristics of market inactivity. The aim of the research is to emphasize the importance of examining capital market characteristics in the valuation process, thereby providing clients with valuations that are relevant and useful for making sound business and investment decisions.

Keywords: *inactive capital market, characteristics of inactivity, value concepts, fair value, valuation methods, discount rate*

---

* *Originally published in 2015 in the Journal Acta Economica, 13(23), pp. 121–138. Reused here with permission from the publisher.*

INTRODUCTION

Theoretical assumptions of many financial models are based on ideal conditions: market liquidity and activity, reliability, relevance and availability of information, informed and willing market participants, market efficiency, and the credibility and auditability of financial statements. In developed market economies, many of these assumptions are feasible, as they are derived from the characteristics of capital markets with decades-long traditions and well-established operational mechanisms.

Valuing a company listed on a developed global stock exchange is not a major challenge, given the availability of both macroeconomic and microeconomic data, market activity, and a high number of comparable transactions and companies. Even private companies in developed market economies can often be evaluated using standardized models and accepted valuation frameworks. However, what happens with companies operating in underdeveloped market economies—and particularly within inactive capital markets?

In such environments, many valuation methods are not applicable. The market approach to valuation, which includes the comparable transactions method and the market multiple method, is extremely difficult to implement when shares of the company being valued are traded only a few times per year. Even if such methods are applied, the valuation outcome will not be considered reliable. Furthermore, in applying the income approach, one major issue is the calculation of beta in the CAPM model for determining the cost of capital, as well as the questionable assumptions underlying cash flow projections.

It is also important to mention the influence of market efficiency on the broader issue of company valuation. A market, even an inefficient one, may value securities more accurately than an appraiser (Mikerević, 2009). Beyond the uncertainty inherent in valuation, another argument in favor of this position is the long-term tendency of market prices to converge with the actual value of a company. Therefore, although it may be argued that markets are not perfectly efficient, there is no definitive evidence that any alternative pricing system would function better (Mikerević, Serdar Raković & Mikerević, 2024). Thus, in this paper, we operate under the assumption of market efficiency, while focusing specifically on the concept of capital market inactivity.

This paper aims to test two hypotheses. The first is that the capital market in the Bosnia and Herzegovina is inactive and underdeveloped. The second hypothesis is that such market inactivity significantly limits and determines the applicability of valuation approaches and methods, the cost of capital, and bases of value. Accordingly, in inactive capital markets, a prerequisite for a relevant company valuation is an examination of the characteristics and dimensions of market inactivity. To support these claims, we will identify and discuss the fundamental characteristics of inactive capital markets, analyze the capital market of the Bosnia and Herzegovina, describe the methodology used in this study, present the research results, and offer concluding views and recommendations on the topic.

1. FUNDAMENTAL CHARACTERISTICS OF INACTIVE CAPITAL MARKETS

According to the International Accounting Standards Board (IASB, Emerging Economies Group, 2011, pp. 8–9), the characteristics of inactive markets include:

- Significant gaps between supply and demand for certain or all securities on the financial market;
- Infrequent buy-sell transactions;
- Absence of market prices;
- Insufficient market depth;
- (Relatively) low market liquidity.

Under Generally Accepted Accounting Principles (GAAP) and Financial Accounting Standards (FAS), an inactive market is one where there are very few buy-sell transactions for the given security or for securities with similar characteristics; where the prices in completed transactions are not current; and where security prices vary significantly over time or between market participants—factors that significantly reduce the relevance of such prices (FASB Staff Position, 2008). By contrast, an active market is a well-developed securities market which, according to the FASB, is characterized by:

- A high volume of transactions;
- Willing and informed buyers and sellers readily available at any time;
- Numerous comparable securities that can be benchmarked against the observed one;
- Relevant prices formed through supply and demand;
- Low transaction costs;
- Reliable and accessible transaction information.

In addition to available pricing and active market participants, an active market also requires the presence of homogenous tradable items (IAS 38 – Intangible Assets).

The (in)activity of a market will inevitably influence the valuation of the company being assessed. Although the valuation process itself is formally the same regardless of market activity, two standard problems arise in the context of inactive markets: *the absence or irrelevance of market prices for either debt or equity*, and *outdated financial statements* that contain fewer important details and more omissions. In such conditions, market value as a fundamental valuation concepts cannot be applied in the same way as it would be on active capital markets. In these cases, the *purpose of the valuation* becomes a key factor in determining company value.

The purpose of the valuation in an inactive market will shape both the valuation procedure and the resulting value. In sale transactions of companies operating within inactive markets, it must be considered that such businesses typically lack diversification. Consequently, valuation models focused solely on undiversified risk may underestimate the discount rate. Furthermore, these investments are illiquid, meaning that illiquidity risk must always be incorporated into the valuation. In inactive markets, the *key person value* often arises (Poznanić & Cvijanović, 2011), indicating that the value includes a strong personal component, where revenues and profit reflect not only operational success but also the presence of the current owner.

In inactive and illiquid capital markets, determining the value of a company is by no means a simple task. The Financial Accounting Standards Board (FASB) in the United States has established a framework for identifying non-regular transactions and determining the fair value of assets and liabilities in inactive markets. The first step is to assess whether the market is indeed inactive; there is a list of factors that a company or investor should evaluate to determine whether there has been a significant decline in volume or activity level for a given asset or liability (FASB Staff Position, 2009):

- There are very few recent transactions;
- Quoted prices are not based on current information;
- Quoted prices vary significantly over time, across different market segments or dealers;
- Indices that were previously highly correlated with the fair values of the assets or liabilities now show clear disconnection from recent fair market value indicators for such assets or liabilities;
- Significant increases in liquidity risk premiums, changes in yields or performance indicators (such as fraud rates or loss severity) observed in transactions or price quotes compared to the enterprise's own cash flow projections, considering all available market data related to credit and other non-performance risks for the asset or liability;
- An unusually wide bid-ask spread or significant increase in this spread;
- A sharp decline or complete absence of a primary market for new issuances of the same or similar assets or liabilities;
- Very limited publicly available information.

Once the first step is completed, the next is to determine whether transactions in an inactive market are *orderly*. Even in an inactive capital market, the appraiser must not automatically assume that all transactions are disorderly. There are specific circumstances that must be evaluated to determine whether a transaction is orderly and whether its inputs are relevant for the purpose of estimating fair value. According to FASB, these include:

- Inadequate market exposure in the period prior to the measurement date to allow for usual and customary marketing activities under current market conditions for the asset or liability;
- The asset or liability was sold by the seller to a single market participant;
- The seller was under duress—facing bankruptcy, receivership, or legal/regulatory pressure that compelled the sale;
- The transaction price is an outlier compared to other recent prices of the same or similar assets or liabilities.

If one or more of the above circumstances is present, the transaction is considered *disorderly*. While a company or appraiser is not obligated to establish whether transactions are orderly, they must not disregard relevant information that is reasonably accessible without incurring disproportionate costs. Transactions that result from forced liquidations or sales under pressure or compulsion cannot be considered relevant for assessing market activity.

It is evident that, in inactive markets, the process of obtaining inputs for valuation is considerably more complex, and the company's value - due to a lack of transparency, limited access to information, and other inherent risks - is less reliable than it would be in active capital markets. Although the FASB guidelines are aimed at determining fair value, they can be equally applied to market value, which is the basis for great number of valuations. What, then, should be done in such conditions? It is essential to analyze how much weight a transaction can carry in determining the fair value of an asset or liability.

If facts indicate that a transaction was not orderly, the appraiser should assign minimal weight to its price when assessing fair value or market risk premium, especially when compared to other indicators. On the other hand, if the transaction is proven to be orderly, the appraiser will consider its price a relevant indicator (FASB Staff Position, 2008).

The degree of importance assigned to transaction prices in comparison with other fair value indicators depends on facts and circumstances such as: the transaction volume, the proximity of the transaction date to the valuation date, and the comparability of the transaction to the asset or liability being measured. If the company or appraiser does not have sufficient information to determine whether transactions were orderly or not, the transaction price will still be considered in estimating fair value and market risk premiums, though it may not be the sole or primary input in the valuation.

Furthermore, if a company uses quoted prices from a third party as inputs for fair value assessment, it must evaluate whether these prices are based on current information that reflects the orderliness of transactions, or on valuation techniques that capture market participant assumptions. When determining the reliability of quoted prices as valuation inputs, less weight will be given to quotes that do not reflect the outcome of actual transactions.

2. THE CAPITAL MARKET IN THE BOSNIA AND HERZEGOVINA

The capital market in Bosnia and Herzegovina is underdeveloped, poorly coordinated, and mainly inactive - a reality confirmed by research conducted by domestic authors. An analysis of data from the Banja Luka and Sarajevo Stock Exchanges indicates that the financial market is underdeveloped in both volume and the number of instruments, multilayered in structure, and dysfunctional. Meanwhile, the banking sector, though moderately developed, is characterized by high representation of basic aggregates, making it more sensitive and risk-prone (Kumalić, 2013).

The state of the financial market is typically measured by the development of its financial structure, the banking sector, the capital market, the relationship between the banking system and the capital market, and the development of non-bank financial intermediaries (Šonje, 2005; as cited in Kumalić, 2013).

In Bosnia and Herzegovina, total financial sector assets amount 52.18 billion KM in 2024. In 2024, banks account for approximately 87.7% of the financial sector, while investment funds held only about 2.2% of total financial assets on average (BLSE, 2024; SASE, 2024). Insurance and reinsurance firms, microcredit organizations and leasing companies accounted for very low shares: 5.4%, 3.4% and 1.3% respectively. The share of brokers & stock exchange in total financial sector assets is negligible, less than 0.3%. Next table shows comparison trend for two periods 2025-2012 and 2012-2024.

Table 1: Comparison Trends: Shares of Different Types of Financial Institutions in Total Financial Sector Assets in Bosnia and Herzegovina

Institution	BIH 2005–2012 (average)	BIH 2012–2024 (average)
Banks	80%	87.6 – 87.7%
Non-bank financial institutions (OFI)	<20%	12.3%
- Insurance & reinsurance	3.8%	5.6%
- Investment funds	5.5%	2.1–2.3%
- Microcredit organisations	3.6%	3.3%
- Leasing companies	5.2%	1.3%
- Brokers & exchanges	negligible	0.3%

Source: CBBA (2024), BLSE (2024), and other CBBA Reports from period 2005-2024.

Comparing two periods, banks have strengthened their dominance, increasing from 80% to nearly 88% of total sector assets. Insurance has grown modestly (from 3.8% to 5.6%). Investment funds have contracted significantly (from 5.5% to 2.2%). Microcredit remains stable (from 3.6% to 3.3%). Leasing has decreased noticeably (from 5.2% to 1.3%). Other non-bank segments remain negligible. The banking sector continues to be the backbone of the financial landscape, with its share rising further. The non-bank financial sector remains underdeveloped, both structurally and in relative scale. Investment funds have diminished significantly. The overall picture remains structurally skewed, showing even more concentration in banking over time. In total observed, the share of non-bank financial institutions is significantly low, below 15%, indicating their insufficient development. Thus, the financial market in Bosnia and Herzegovina is structurally underdeveloped.

Table 2: Historic Comparison: Financial sector structure in Bosnia and Herzegovina and EU for period 2005-2024

Indicator	BiH (2005–2012) (average)	EU (2005–2012) (average)	BiH (2012–2024) (average)	EU (2012–2024) (average)
Banking sector share of financial assets	80%	60-70%	87.6% (2024)	55-65% (varies across EU-27)
Investment funds	5.5%	15-25%	2.2%	20-30%
Insurance	3.8%	6-10%	5.6%	7-11%
Leasing & microcredit institutions (combined)	8-9%	5-10%	4.6%	4-9%

Source: European Central Bank (2024), Eurostat (2024), OECD (2023), European Banking Federation. (2024).

Compared to EU average, *Bosnia and Herzegovina remains bank-dominated*, unlike the EU where capital markets and investment funds play a stronger role. Non-bank financial institutions (NBFIs) in the EU steadily grew or diversified post-crisis, while in BiH they either stagnated or declined in share. Capital market depth in BiH remains significantly below EU levels, where even smaller markets like Slovenia or Croatia have achieved higher ratios. The EU's financial structure has shifted toward more capital market-based financing, especially post-2010, under initiatives like the *Capital Markets Union*. BiH's market has remained structurally inert by comparison. Comparing latest information, capital market debt indicators in Bosnia and Herzegovina differ from the average data for EU. BIH Turnover-to-GDP (SASE / BLSE) is approximately 3.7% of GDP (for 2023) and BIH market capitalization / GDP is in range 25-30%. Turnover-to-GDP in EU is between 70–100% and Market capitalisation/GDP is between 50-60 %.

According to the EBRD Transition Report 2024–25, Bosnia and Herzegovina's financial sector assets amounted to approximately 105% of GDP in 2023. The ratio of financial sector assets to GDP in Bosnia and Herzegovina ranges between 89% and 112.4% in period 2025-2012, and 95% to 121% in period 2012–2024. In the first observed period the peak was in 2007 at 112.4%, and in the second period - in 2019 at 121% (pre-COVID expansion). The indicators demonstrate that the banking sector is by far the most developed part of Bosnia and Herzegovina's financial market. In developed countries, the ratio of banking sector assets to GDP often exceeds 100%, and in some cases reaches as high as 150% (Kumalić, 2013).

Determining the Discount Rate

When determining discount rates in inactive markets, undiversified risk alone is not sufficient. Conventional financial models of risk and return assume that marginal investors in companies are diversified and therefore concerned only with non-diversifiable risk. This type of risk is measured using beta, typically estimated from historical data on prices and returns. In inactive markets, it is more appropriate to use so-called *bottom-up betas* to derive an unlevered beta (Beneda, 2003).

The total unlevered beta measures all risk as the ratio of market beta to the correlation between the company and the market (Damodaran, 2012). This approach reveals how much of the company's risk stems from market factors versus firm-specific risk. The final step in beta estimation is to determine the debt-to-equity ratio and calculate the cost of equity. The *levered beta* is calculated by applying the debt-to-equity ratio to the unlevered beta. Thus, the levered beta represents the beta for an equity investment in the company, reflecting both business risk and the financial leverage level (Fernández, 2006). For calculating the cost of capital, the same industry-average debt ratio used to lever the beta is applied.

In addition to the discount rate issue, the *effect of illiquidity* must also be analyzed - an ever-present factor in inactive capital markets. Market liquidity, as a crucial element in capital market investment decisions, provides security to investors and reduces the risk that they will be unable to exit their positions without substantial losses in asset value (Yeyati, Schmukler & van Horen, 2007). Liquidity is considered a fundamental driver of capital market development. Generally, liquidity depends on the presence of a large number of buyers and sellers at all times, the ability to execute the next transaction at a similar price to the previous one, and the market's capacity to absorb the purchase or sale of larger volumes of securities without significantly affecting prices (Benić & Franić, 2008, p. 483).

Moreover, larger companies with better performance and more liquid assets will face lower liquidity discounts compared to smaller, loss-making firms. Liquidity becomes especially critical during periods of economic recession, rather than during times of growth. It is also significantly more important to short-term investors—those with shorter investment horizons and greater immediate cash needs—than to long-term investors who are willing to hold their investments over time.

3. METHODOLOGICAL FRAMEWORK OF THE ANALYSIS

The inactivity and illiquidity of capital markets, and their impact on the procedure and process of company valuation, have been the subject of numerous international studies and publications (Damodaran, 2012; Pereiro, 2002; Lesmond, 2005; Bekaert, Harvey & Lundblad, 2005). Relevant information regarding transaction regularity and market inactivity is found in research conducted by the FASB and IASB. Studies on the causes of the 2007–2008 financial crisis, conducted by the International Valuation Standards Council (IVSC), concluded that during the pre-crisis period, investors often placed excessive trust in company valuations based on inactive and dysfunctional markets.

The characteristics of inactive capital markets influence the company valuation process, the selection of valuation approaches and methods, and the choice of models for determining the discount rate. The aim of this research is to highlight the importance of analyzing capital market characteristics within the valuation process, so that the results provided to clients are relevant and useful for making sound business and investment decisions.

For the purposes of this study, we used data obtained through a survey of 78 certified appraisers in period 2015-2016 in Bosnia and Herzegovina, all of whom held valid licenses for conducting valuations. Most of the questions were closed-ended: direct questions, multiple-choice questions, and intensity-based response options. Respondents were asked to identify the characteristics of capital market inactivity that they believe are present in the Bosnia and Herzegovina. They were also asked to indicate which value concepts they use in their appraisals, the approaches and methods they most frequently apply, and the model they use for determining the cost of capital. The survey was limited to examining capital market inactivity in the Bosnia and Herzegovina.

The results of other studies compared with our own confirm our hypotheses. We also used data from the Banja Luka Stock Exchange, the Sarajevo Stock Exchange, reports from the Central Bank, the Statistical Office of the Republic of Srpska, as well as data from studies by the World Bank, FASB, IASB, and IVSC.

4. RESEARCH RESULTS

The research results indicate a high level of agreement among respondents with the assertion that the capital market in our country is inactive and underdeveloped. Research was done in 2015-2016 in Bosnia and Herzegovina. Of the 78 respondents, 94% believe that the capital market in the Bosnia and Herzegovina is inactive, while 6% did not answer the question. None of the respondents stated that the capital market in our country is active.

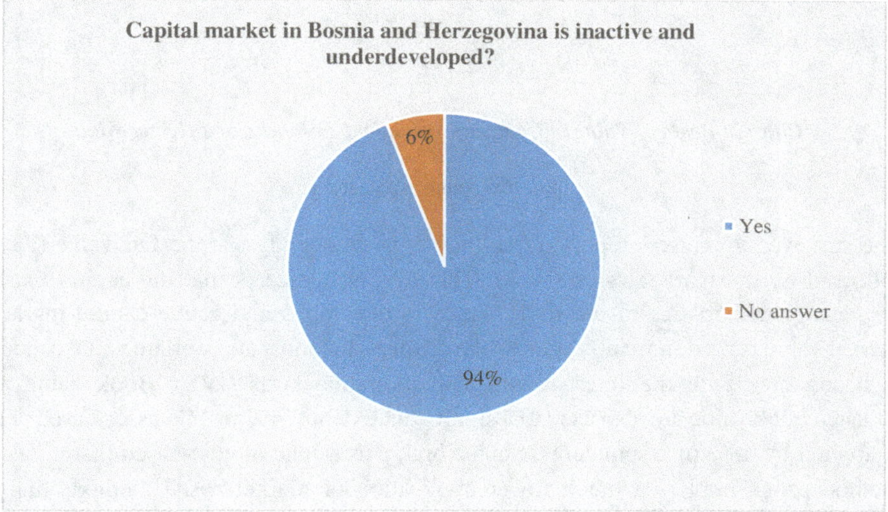

Chart 1: Capital Market Inactivity in Bosnia and Herzegovina

Source: Author's research

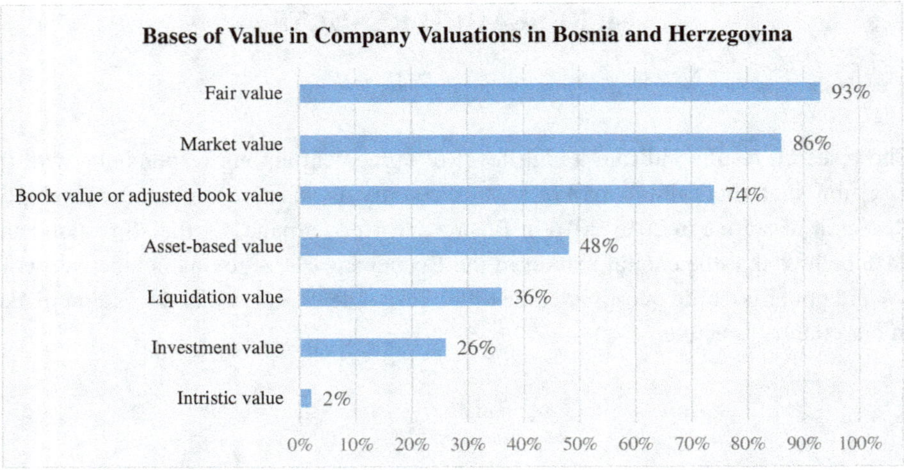

Chart 2: Bases of Value in Company Valuations in Bosnia and Herzegovina

Source: Author's research

The surveyed appraisers reported that they most frequently use the fair value (93%), followed by the market value (86%). This finding indicates that the capital market displays characteristics of inactivity, since in developed and active capital markets, market value is predominantly used as the primary and most appropriate value concept, in accordance with the International Valuation Standards (IVS). Book value and adjusted book value are also used to a significant extent (74%), while asset-based value is applied by 48% of respondents. Such a high percentage of cost-based (asset-based) method usage implies a much lower application of market-based methods than is typical in active capital markets. Liquidation value is used by 36% of respondents, while investment value, as a more specific concept, is applied by 26%. Intrinsic value is used in a negligible number of cases (2%), likely due to the difficulties in defining and applying this concept in practice.

Thus, the research results confirm the hypothesis that the capital market in the Bosnia and Herzegovina is underdeveloped and exhibits, to varying degrees, all the typical features associated with market inactivity.

Since market inactivity significantly influences the choice of valuation approaches and methods and given the known challenges in defining inputs for certain methods, we analysed the extent to which appraisers in the Bosnia and Herzegovina use individual methods and how much importance they assign to them. The *valuation method significance scale* ranges from 1 to 5, as follows:

1 – not used in valuations,
2 – not important,
3 – of minor importance,
4 – moderately important,
5 – very important in the valuation process.

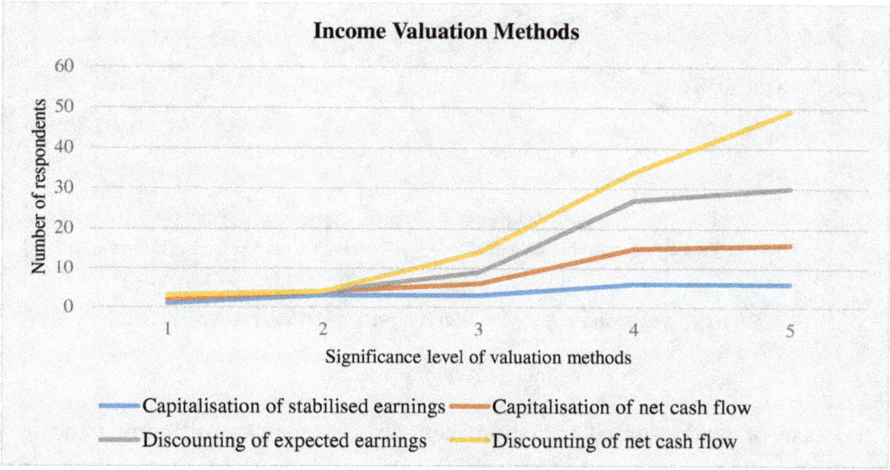

Chart 3: Importance Level of Income Methods in Valuations

Source: Author's research

The most frequently used and most highly regarded method is the discounted cash flow (DCF) method. The largest share of respondents (nearly 40%) consider this method to be very important. Not a single respondent stated that they do not use the DCF method or consider it unimportant. The *discounted expected earnings method* is also used in a significant number of valuations, although by somewhat fewer respondents than the DCF method. 28% of respondents consider this method to be very important. The *capitalisation of net cash flow* method was deemed moderately important by 18% of respondents, and very important by 20%. Finally, due to its application limitations, the *capitalisation of stabilised earnings method* is the least frequently used; only 12% of respondents consider it very important in the business valuation process.

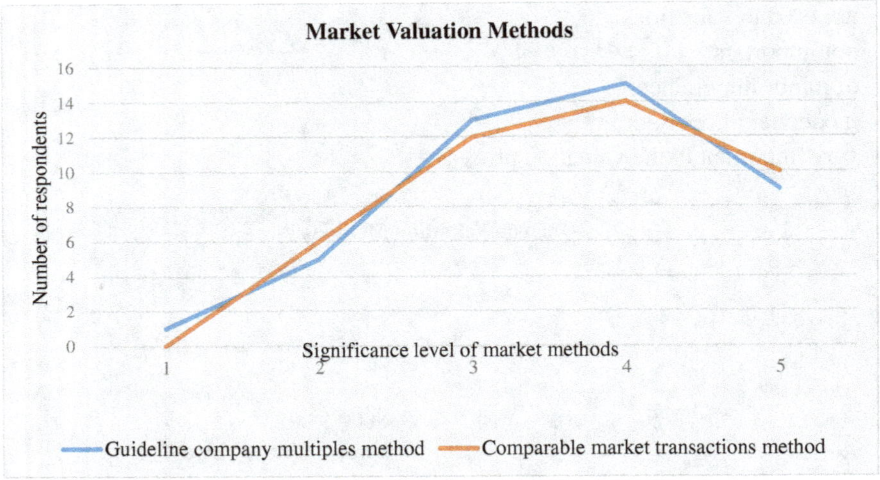

Chart 4: Importance Level of Market-Based Methods in Valuations

Source: Author's research

In the case of market-based valuation methods, a somewhat different trend in the importance scale is observed. The central portion of the chart contains the highest concentration of responses, indicating that cumulatively, the majority of respondents consider market-based methods to be of moderate or lesser importance. 28% of respondents rated the *comparable transactions method* as moderately important, while 30% assigned the same level of importance to the *guideline company multiples method***.** Approximately one-quarter of respondents rated both methods as less important. On the other hand, a high level of importance was attributed to market methods by 18% (for the multiples method) and 20% (for the comparable transactions method). It is notable that nearly 40% of respondents did not provide an answer regarding the use of market-based approaches.

Compared to *discounting methods* (discounted cash flow and discounted expected earnings), it is clear that *market-based methods are used less frequently*. The general level of importance for both market-based methods is moderate, suggesting that appraisers would make greater use of them if market conditions - particularly in terms of activity - were aligned with the requirements of the market approach.

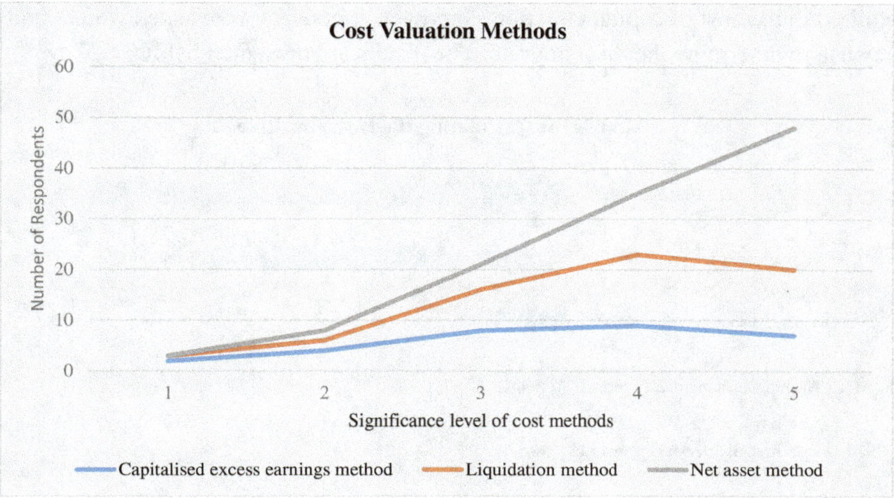

Chart 5: Importance Level of Cost-Based Methods in Valuations

Source: Author's research

The chart shows that the most frequently used method is the *net asset method*, which 56% of respondents rated as very important, while 25% considered it moderately important in the valuation process. A smaller share of respondents (10%) stated that they consider the net asset method to be less important. The *liquidation method* was rated as very important by 26%, and moderately important by 28% of respondents—reflecting its practical relevance, especially given that bankruptcy cases are relatively frequent in Bosnia and Herzegovina, making the liquidation method essential in such contexts. The *capitalised excess earnings method* is the least frequently used; cumulatively, most respondents rated it as moderately important (18%) or less important (16%). Only 14% of respondents consider this method to be very important.

The high level of importance assigned to asset-based methods, compared to market-based methods, further indicates that the capital market in the Bosnia and Herzegovina is inactive. These results are consistent with research conducted in other inactive capital markets (Lesmond, 2005; Yeyati, Schmukler & Van Horen, 2007), where asset-based methods are also most commonly used, followed by income-based valuation methods.

Finally, when selecting a model for determining the cost of capital, challenges arise not only in calculating beta in the CAPM model, but also in defining other inputs required in the cost of capital equation. Surveyed appraisers were asked which models they use to determine the discount rate. The results are presented below.

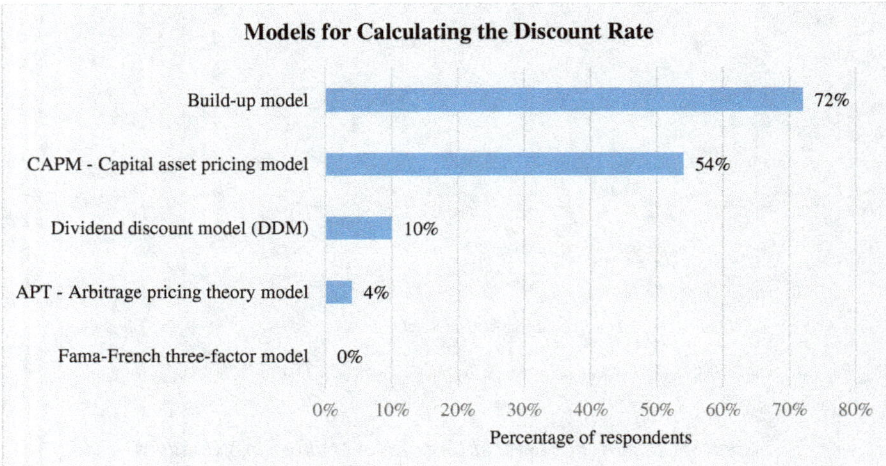

Chart 6: Frequency of Use of Discount Rate Calculation Models

Source: Author's research

Valuers in the Bosnia and Herzegovina predominantly use the *Build-up model* (72%), which correlates with the condition of the capital market. The Build-up model, in addition to the risk-free rate, includes some or all of the following components: equity risk premium, size premium, and company-specific risk premium. It may also incorporate a country risk premium, reflecting political and economic instability—an attribute typical of inactive capital markets (Pratt &Grabowski, 2008, p. 70).

Difficulties in determining the inputs for the CAPM model, especially the beta coefficient as a measure of systematic risk, complicate its application in inactive markets; 54% of surveyed appraisers report using this model. In contrast, on active capital markets, CAPM remains the most commonly used approach for estimating the cost of capital, as it reflects the economic principle that the company is one of many possible investment alternatives on the market and should therefore be valued according to the same principles governing other investment assets.

The *Dividend discount model* (DDM) is used by only 10% of respondents, primarily due to the lack of a consistent dividend payment practice in the Bosnia and Herzegovina. The *Arbitrage pricing theory* (APT) model, which assumes the presence of multiple risk factors, is used by just 4% of respondents. Its limited application, even in developed markets, stems from the absence of consensus on which variables should be included for optimal explanatory power. Likewise, the *Fama-French three-factor model* is not used at all in the Bosnia and Herzegovina, likely due to the challenges of integrating additional market variables in an environment with limited data availability.

It can therefore be concluded that the second hypothesis is also confirmed: cost-based (asset-based) and income-based methods dominate in valuation practice, while market-based approaches are marginalised. Additionally, the Build-up model is the dominant method for calculating discount rates.

CONCLUSION

Inactive markets are not a phenomenon exclusive to developing countries - they are also found within developed market economies, where certain segments or even entire markets may experience inactivity. In response to this, the FASB provides guidance for valuers, auditors, and investors on how to estimate fair value when market activity is significantly reduced and transactions are infrequent or irregular.

In such conditions, the market value may no longer be relevant, and alternative value bases, particularly fair value, have to be employed. It becomes essential to assess the regularity of transactions to determine whether the inputs used for fair value estimation are reliable. If a transaction is deemed irregular, the valuer should assign it minimal weight. Conversely, a verified regular transaction may serve as a valid price indicator. When there is insufficient information to determine regularity, the transaction price may still be considered but should not be the sole or primary factor. Regarding discount rate determination, undiversified risk alone is insufficient in inactive markets. The use of so-called build-up betas is necessary, along with a careful consideration of the illiquidity effect, which is a common consequence of capital market inactivity. Liquidity is, after all, a foundational condition for the development of a functional capital market.

The research findings confirm that the capital market in the Bosnia and Herzegovina exhibits most, if not all, characteristics of illiquidity. The second hypothesis is thereby affirmed: market inactivity significantly limits and determines the choice of valuation approaches, methods, discount rate models, and value concepts. Among valuation methods, cost-based are used most frequently, followed by income-based approaches, while market-based methods are rarely applied. In the domain of discount rate estimation, the Build-up model is dominant, followed by CAPM.

Under such conditions, substantial adjustments or even replacement of market-based valuation methods are recommended. In cases where transactions are not regular, market inputs may need to be disregarded altogether. The ability to assess transaction relevance and properly adjust market data is crucial for delivering reliable and representative valuation outcomes on inactive capital markets - valuations that reflect the most realistic figure within a reasonable range of fair value estimates.

REFERENCES

Banja Luka Stock Exchange (BLSE). (2024). *Annual Statistical Bulletin.* https://www.blberza.com

Bosnia and Herzegovina Transition Report (2024-2025). *Country Assessment.* file:///C:/Users/pc/Downloads/TransitionReport202425BosniaandHerzegovina.pdf

Bekaert G., Harvey C. R., & Lundblad, C. (2005). Liquidity and Expected Returns: Lessons from Emerging Markets. *National Bureau of Economic Research.* Working Paper, No. 11413. http://www.nber.org/papers/w11413

Beneda, N. L. (2003). Estimating Cost of Capital Using Bottom-up Betas. *CPA Journal*, *73*(5), 66-71.

Benić, V., & Franić, I. (2008). Komparativna analiza likvidnosti tržišta kapitala Hrvatske i zemalja regije. *Financijska teorija i praksa*, *32*(4), 481-502.

Central Bank of Bosnia and Herzegovina (CBBA). (2024). *Financial Stability Report 2023–2024*. CBBiH, Sarajevo. https://www.cbbh.ba

Damodaran, A. (2012). *Investment Valuation: Tools and Techniques for Determining the Value of Any Asset.* John Wiley and Sons, 3rd edition.

European Banking Federation. (2024). *EBF Facts and Figures 2024*. EBF, Brussels. https://www.ebf.eu

European Central Bank. (2024). *Consolidated banking data – EU and euro area banking sector statistics.* https://www.ecb.europa.eu/stats/financial_corporations/consolidated/html/index.en.html

European Insurance and Occupational Pensions Authority (EIOPA). (2024). *Financial Stability Report – June 2024*. EIOPA, Frankfurt. https://www.eiopa.europa.eu

Eurostat. (2024). *Financial balance sheets by institutional sector - EU aggregate data (2023).* https://ec.europa.eu/eurostat

IASB. Emerging Economies Group. (2011). *Guidelines on the apllication of the fair value measurement standard in emerging economies*. http://www.ifrs.org/The-organisation/Advisory-bodies/EEG/Documents/EEG-meeting-July-2011.pdf

Intereconomics / Centre for European Policy Studies (CEPS). (2023). Are the Commission's Plans Enough to Build Deep and Integrated Capital Markets in the EU? *Intereconomics, 58*(5), 262–266. https://doi.org/10.1007/s10272-023-1079-4

International Valuation Standards Council (IVSC). (2009). *Valuation in Markets Unaffected by Disorderly Conditions*. IVSC, London.

IVSC. (2025). *International Valuation Standards*. https://ivsc.org

Yeyati, L. E., Schmukler, S. L., & Van Horen, N. (2007). *Emerging Market Liquidity and Crises. Policy Research Working Paper, 4445.* The World Bank. http://wwwwds.worldbank.org/external/default/WDSContentServer/WDSP/IB/2007/12/13/000158349_20071213152426/Rendered/PDF/wps4445.pdf

Kumalić, I. (2013). Razvijenost finansijskog tržišta u Bosni i Hercegovini. *Časopis za ekonomiju i tržišne komunikacije*, *3*(1), 57-72. https://doi.org/10.7251/EMC1301057K

Lesmond, D. A. (2005). Liquidity of Emerging Markets. *Journal of Financial Economics, 77*(2), 411-452. https://doi.org/10.1016/j.jfineco.2004.01.005

Mikerević, D. (2009). *Principi i praksa procjene vrijednosti preduzeća*. Finrar Banja Luka.

Mikerević, D., Serdar Raković, T., & Mikerević, D. (2024). *Principi i praksa procjene vrijednosti.* Finrar doo Banja Luka.

OECD. (2023). *Institutional Investors Statistics: Assets and Liabilities of Investment Funds and Insurance Corporations*. OECD. Stat. https://stats.oecd.org

Pereiro, L. (2002). *Valuation of Companies in Emerging Markets: A Practical Approach.* John Wiley and Sons

Poznanić, V., Cvijanović, J. M. (2011). *Metode vrednovanja preduzeća*. Ekonomski institut, Beograd.

Pratt, S. (2008). *Cost of Capital: Estimation and Applications.* John Wiley and Sons

FASB Staff Position. (2008). FAS no. 157-3. *Determining the fair value of a financial asset when the market for that asset is not active*. Financial Accounting Foundation. http://www.fasb.org/jsp/FASB/Document_C/DocumentPage?cid=1218220135667&acceptedDisclaimer=true

FASB Staff Position. (2009). FAS no. 157-e. *Determining Whether a Market Is Not Active and a Transaction Is Not Distressed.* USA: Financial Accounting Foundation. http://www.fasb.org/jsp/FASB/Document_C/DocumentPage?cid=1176154537247&acceptedDisclaimer=true

Fernández, P. (2006). Levered and unlevered beta. *Working Paper, WP no 488*, January 2003, Rev. May 2006. http://www.iese.edu/research/pdfs/DI-0488-E.pdf

Sarajevo Stock Exchange (SASE). (2024). *Market Statistics Reports*. https://www.sase.ba

Statistical Office of Republika Srpska. (2024). *Annual Bulletin of Financial Statistics*. https://www.rzs.rs.ba

Šonje, V. (2005). Veza koja nedostaje: Kako povezati razvoj tržžišta kapitala i gospodarski rast. Arhivanalitika, Zagreb.

World Bank. (2023). *Financial Sector Assessment Bosnia and Herzegovina*. https://www.worldbank.org

IV [*]THE USE OF DISCOUNTS AND PREMIUMS IN APPRAISALS OF COMPANIES

Abstract

With the accelerated development of capital markets during the 20th century and the increasing prevalence of joint-stock companies in practice, the use of discounts and premiums has gained growing importance. The value of a company, as well as the applied discounts, is observed from two perspectives: majority interest (enterprise-level discounts) and minority interest (shareholder-level discounts). Enterprise-level discounts affect the value of the company as a whole and are applied to the control-level value, while shareholder-level discounts - such as the discount for lack of control and the discount for lack of marketability - apply to specific groups of shareholders, particularly minority shareholders. These two discounts have a significant effect on the resulting business value. The aim of this research is to highlight the state of valuation practice in the Bosnia and Herzegovina, with regard to the importance and frequency of applying discounts and premiums in business valuation. The results indicate that the majority of surveyed appraisers in the Bosnia and Herzegovina primarily assess the majority interest, while the analysis of minority interest has a somewhat lower level of application in practice. The use of control premiums, as well as discounts for lack of control and lack of marketability, will naturally result in differing valuation outcomes for majority and minority shareholders. The application of discounts and premiums requires a high level of professional judgment, strong analytical engagement, and a deep understanding of the subject matter. Nonetheless, they remain an indispensable part of business valuation in order to ensure that the final estimated value reflects the real situation, depending on whether the valuation is conducted from a majority or minority interest perspective.

Keywords: *Discount for lack of control, discount for lack of marketability, control premium, business valuation, estimated value.*

---

[*] *Originally published in 2015 in the Journal Financing, 6(4), pp. 35–43. Reused here with permission from the publisher.*

INTRODUCTION

The globalization of the world economy, the growing mobility of capital, and the current geopolitical landscape have introduced new challenges in business valuation practices and the application of valuation results for better-informed business decisions. Increasing company value has become a condition for market survival, making the definition and determination of objective and realistic company value crucial. Consequently, the issue of business valuation has taken a central role in analysis, strategic planning, and the development of modern enterprises.

Alongside core valuation parameters and value concepts, the purpose of valuation strongly shapes the process and its outcome, particularly in terms of the ownership perspective from which the valuation is approached. In both academic and professional discourse, there is notable interest in analyzing value differences between majority and minority shareholders. The calculation of discounts and premiums represents the final stage of the valuation process, leaving a decisive imprint on the appraised value by answering a key question: Is the valuation being conducted for a majority or minority shareholder?

Company value may be viewed in two ways: as the value of the majority owner (control value), and as the value attributed to minority shareholders (minority marketable value, or equivalent to public market value of shares). Therefore, discounts can likewise be classified into two broad categories:

- *Company-level discounts*, which apply to all shareholders and affect the value of the company as a whole, typically applied to the value of the controlling interest;
- *Shareholder-level discounts*, such as discount for lack of control and discount for lack of marketability, which pertain to a specific group of shareholders, typically minority shareholders or those lacking voting rights. These shareholder-level discounts are applied after enterprise-level adjustments.

This paper begins from the hypothesis that the application of discounts and premiums results in different appraised values for majority and minority shareholders, and that such adjustments are essential for ensuring that the appraised value reflects the real condition of the company from the appropriate ownership perspective. The objective of this research is to assess the state of the valuation profession in the Bosnia and

Herzegovina regarding the importance and frequency of using discounts and premiums in business valuations.

In the following sections, we will examine the theoretical foundations for calculating discounts and premiums in business valuation, including the quantitative model of marketability discount. We will address the practical use of discounts, especially the discount for illiquidity in private company valuations. The methodology of our research will be presented, followed by an analysis of the results obtained in the Bosnia and Herzegovina, and finally, we will offer conclusions regarding the application of discounts and premiums in valuation practice.

1. THEORETICAL FOUNDATIONS FOR CALCULATING DISCOUNTS AND PREMIUMS

With the rapid development of capital markets throughout the 20th century and the growing prevalence of joint-stock companies in practice, the use of discounts and premiums has gained considerable importance. Depending on whether the valuation is approached from a control or minority interest perspective, discounts are classified into two general categories.

Enterprise-level discounts, applied to the control-level value, include the following (Pratt, 2009):

- Discount for trapped capital gains;
- Key person discount;
- Discount for known or potential environmental liabilities;
- Discount for pending litigation;
- Discount for portfolio, conglomerate, or non-homogeneous (unattractive) assets;
- Discount for customer or supplier concentration.

These adjustments may be embedded in the discount or capitalisation rate in income approaches, or in the multiples used in market approaches. In either case, they must be clearly disclosed and justified.

Shareholder-level discounts include (Pratt, 2009):

- Discount for lack of control;
- Discount for lack of marketability.

Other shareholder-level discounts include those applied to non-voting shares or block shareholdings. All discounts and premiums are applied after the base valuation process is complete. In light of this classification, two broad groups of valuation methods emerge:

I *Methods for valuing the majority shareholder interest* include all standard approaches: market, cost, and income (Mikerević, 2009). The highest of these values (whether market, asset, or income-based) is considered the control value.

II *Methods for valuing minority shareholder* interests fall into direct and indirect approaches.

According to Pratt (2009), *direct methods* include:

- Analysis of discounted future benefits;
- Capitalization of minority shareholder benefits at an appropriate rate;
- Past transactions;
- Negotiated sale commissions.

Indirect methods involve deducting the discount for lack of control and the discount for lack of marketability from the previously determined control value.

According to the International Glossary of Business Valuation Terms (AICPA, 2012), *marketability* refers to the ability to sell a given asset, while *liquidity* refers to the speed at which an asset can be converted into cash without significant loss in value. In valuation contexts, these terms are often used interchangeably. Thus, marketability or liquidity is defined as the ability to convert ownership interests into cash quickly and with minimal transaction costs, at a price close to the observable market value (Pratt, 2009, p. 7).

A discount or premium is warranted when the characteristics of value relevant to a particular party (majority or minority shareholder) differ from the characteristics of the base value to which the adjustment is applied. Discounts and premiums quantify this difference. According to the Business Valuation Standards (ASA, 2009, Standard VII), the need to apply such adjustments may arise from: the purpose of the valuation, the valuation standard being applied, or other specific circumstances.

The control premium reflects the value of control, representing the amount by which the pro rata value of a controlling interest exceeds that of a minority interest (AICPA, 2012).

The following chart illustrates levels of value based on different ownership interests in a company.

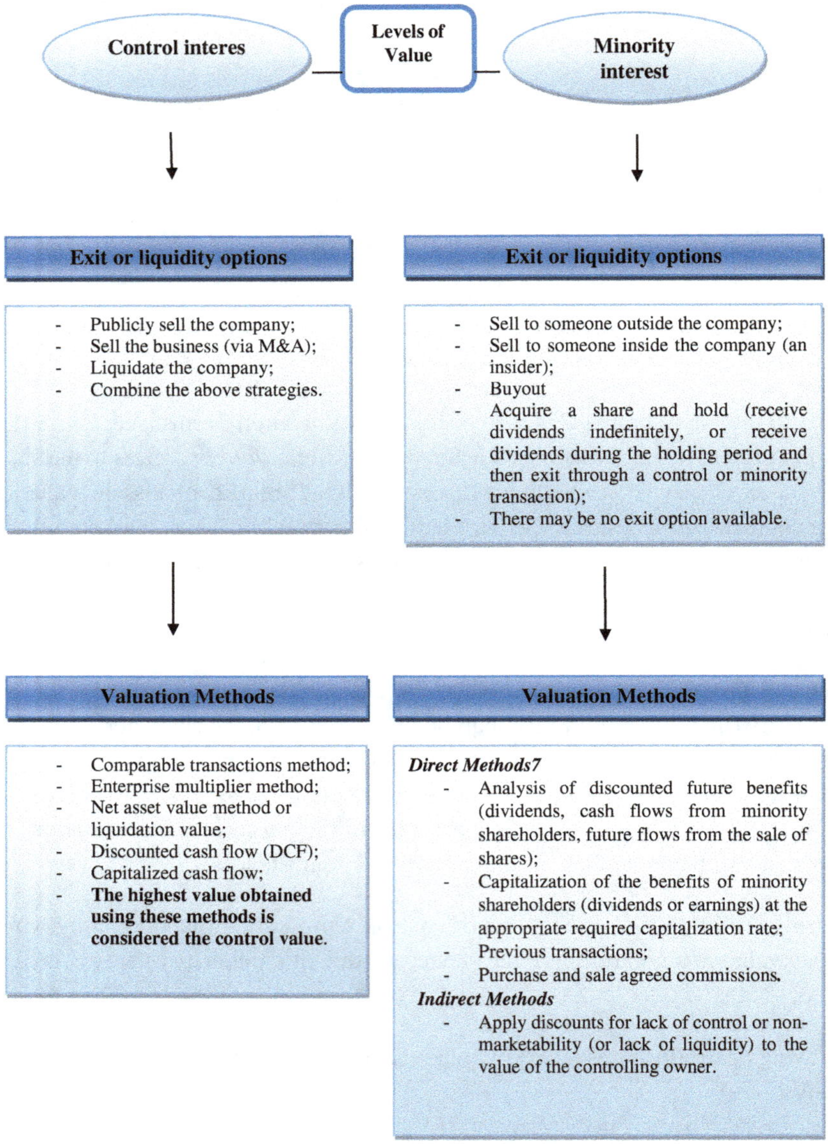

Chart 1: Value Levels Based on Ownership Interest

Source: Pratt, 2009, p.6.

Example 1: Indirect Methods for Valuing Minority Shareholders (according to Pratt, 2009)

Let us assume that the control value of a company's share is \$10. This is the value of the share held by the majority owner, and it includes the control premium. *The question arises: how to determine the value of a minority shareholder's share that is not marketable?*

From the control value of the share (\$10), we subtract the minority interest discount (20%, for example):

$$\$10 – (20\% \times \$10) = \$10 - \$2 = \$8$$

The minority interest discount is essentially a discount for lack of control by minority shareholders. This \$8 represents the value of a minority shareholder's share that is marketable (a marketable minority interest). However, if the minority interest is non-marketable, that fact must also be reflected in the calculation. Now we subtract the marketability discount (45%) from the \$8 value of the minority shareholder's share:

$$\$8 – (45\% \times \$8) = \$8 - \$3.60 = \$4.40$$

The share value of \$4.40 is the value of a minority shareholder's share that is non-marketable (non-marketable minority interest). This share value of \$4.40 represents the share value reduced by: the discount for lack of control (\$2) and the discount for lack of marketability (\$3.60).

Thus, the most significant discounts at the shareholder level are the discount for lack of control and the discount for lack of marketability. The discount for lack of control can be applied to all ownership stakes below 51%. According to Shaw (2014), some authors, based on studies in the USA, suggest this discount ranges from 20-60%, although in practice the boundaries are not strict.

The criteria for determining the marketability discount in the USA include revenue levels, operating income, the analysis period, industry rank (in the USA: SIC or NAICS code), and the types of securities issued by the company (Pratt, 2009). The marketability discount can be applied not only to minority interests but also to control interests, if the control interest is insufficiently marketable (DiMattia, 2008), but only in specific circumstances. For example, these discounts may be relevant if the company is private, has limited growth opportunities, if its earnings are subject to significant risk, if the transfer of earnings and shares is restricted, or if no public market for the company exists.

The factors influencing the size of the marketability discount can be divided into several groups (Pratt, 2009, p. 187):

- size of distributions (dividends, payouts);
- liquidity outlook (the likely holding period for the securities);
- pool of potential buyers (which affects the liquidity outlook);
- risk factors (that influence the expected rate of return during the holding period, i.e., the discount rate);
- growth prospects (which affect the potential selling price, i.e., the residual value of the company).

In addition to these, it is also important to mention the discount for blocks of shares (Pratt, 2009, p. 119). According to Black's Law Dictionary (Garner, 2014), "*blockage*" refers to the recognition in tax valuation that large blocks of shares may not be sold and converted to cash as quickly as smaller quantities of shares. Thus, this is a discount applied to the price of large blocks of shares. It typically involves shares that do not represent a controlling interest in the corporation. The block rule is that blocks of shares are valued lower than the aggregate value of individual shares due to the difficulty of selling such a block at full price (Garner, 2014).

2. QUANTITATIVE MARKETABILITY DISCOUNT MODEL

The Quantitative Marketability Discount Model (QMDM) is a discounted cash flow model at the shareholder level. It is a two-stage model used to estimate value within the income approach. It provides a standardized form for analyzing, projecting, and discounting relevant shareholder cash flows and is applicable to any non-marketable minority interest of a business entity. The model's inputs are the same as in the traditional discounted cash flow model at the enterprise level: cash flows, discount rate, and long-term growth rate. The structure of the DCF model at the shareholder level is shown below (Pratt, 2009, p. 214):

Two-Stage Discounted Cash Flow Model at the Company Level

$$V_e = \sum_{i=1}^{f}\left(\frac{CF(1+g_e)^i}{(1+r)^i}\right) + \left(\frac{CF(1+g_e)^{(f+1)}/(r-g)}{(1+r)^f}\right)$$

PVICF **PVTV**

V_e – value of the company;

r – riskiness of cash flows, i.e., discount rate at the enterprise level;

CF – cash flow to the enterprise;

F – number of years (i= 1, f);

g_e – temporary growth rate;

g – long-term growth rate;

PVICF – present value of interim cash flows during the final projected period ending in year f;

PVTV – present value of the residual, i.e., terminal value of the company.

Two-Stage Discounted Cash Flow Model at the Shareholder Level

$$V_e = \sum_{i=1}^{f} \left(\frac{CF_{sh}(1+g_d)^i}{(1+R_{hp})^i} \right) + \left(\frac{V_e(1+g_v)^f(1+P/D\%)}{(1+R_{hp})^f} \right)$$

PVICF **PVTV**

V_e – value of the company;

V_{sh} – shareholder-level value (value for minority shareholders);

f – expected holding period of the equity interest (securities);

CF_{sh} – expected shareholder cash flow ($CF_{sh} < CF$);

g_d – annual growth rate;

g_v – assumed growth rate during the holding period of the equity interest (in this case, shares);

P/D – potential premium / discount;

R_{hp} – expected return during the holding period of the share, i.e., discount rate ($R_{hp} > R$);

i – year in which shareholders expect to receive cash flows.

Based on the above, we can calculate the *marketability discount (MD).*

$$MD = 1 - \frac{V_{sh}}{V_e}$$

where: V_e – value of the company, V_{sh} –shareholder-level value (value for minority shareholders).

The marketability discount is not an input, but rather the result of a business valuation. The shareholder-level discount rate is a component of the company-level discount rate and represents a holding period premium required to compensate the minority shareholder for assuming additional risk when investing in a non-marketable share. Minority shareholders face additional risks such as: uncertainty about the expected holding period, restrictions on the transfer of funds, potential exposure to so-called adverse cash flows (e.g., if the company fails to receive tax benefits), and so on.

Furthermore, any combination of agency costs and incremental shareholder risks contributes to the reduction of V_{sh} compared to V_e, thereby increasing the marketability discount (MD). The model assumes that all enterprise cash flows are either distributed or reinvested at the enterprise's discount rate, i.e., its cost of capital. Suboptimal investment lowers the expected value growth, and thus V_{sh} implies a higher marketability discount.

This model, within the integrated theory, explores the relationship between company-level value and shareholder-level value. QMDM is a discounted cash flow model at the shareholder level, standardized to express the value of nearly all non-marketable minority interests. As noted by Pratt (2009), non-marketable minority interests generally have lower value than the proportional share of enterprise value due to a combination of agency costs (which affect both the discount rate and the growth of cash flows) and incremental risk during the holding period, which leads to a required return during the holding period that exceeds the enterprise-level discount rate.

Example 2: Calculating the marketability discount using QMDM (according to Pratt, 2009).

Let us assume the following.

Table 1: Model QMDM on example

<table>
<tr><td colspan="3">Expected holding period of the share</td><td>10 years</td></tr>
<tr><td colspan="3">Expected dividend yield</td><td>10%</td></tr>
<tr><td colspan="3">Expected dividend growth rate</td><td>5%</td></tr>
<tr><td colspan="3">Timing convention (end or mid-year)</td><td>End of the year</td></tr>
<tr><td colspan="3">Growth in value during the holding period of the share</td><td>5%</td></tr>
<tr><td colspan="3">Premium / discount for the projected enterprise value</td><td>0%</td></tr>
<tr><td colspan="3">Expected return during the holding period</td><td>20%</td></tr>
<tr><td colspan="4">Company value (in millions of $) by year will be:</td></tr>
<tr><td colspan="4">0 1 2 3 4 5 6 7 8 9 10</td></tr>
<tr><td colspan="4">|$1.000 | $1.050 | $1.103 | $1.158 | $1.216 | $1.276 | $1.340 | $1.407 | $1.477 | $1.551 | $1.629|</td></tr>
<tr><td colspan="4">Discount Period | 1 | 2 | 3 | 4 | 5 | 6 | 7 | 8 | 9 | 10 |</td></tr>
<tr><td colspan="4">Present value |0.8333 |0.6944 |0.5787 |0.4823 |0.4019 |0.3349|0.2791 |0.2326| 0.1938 |0.1615|
Factors of cash flow – PVICF</td></tr>
<tr><td colspan="4">Present value factor |0.1615|
(terminal value) – PVTV</td></tr>
<tr><td colspan="3">Nonmarketable minority value (NMV)</td><td>Present value of cash flows by year and residual value</td></tr>
<tr><td>PVICF</td><td>$0.491</td><td>65.1%</td><td>|$0.083| $0.073| $0.064|$0.056|$0.049 |$0.043 |$0.037 |$0.033 |$0.029| $0.025|</td></tr>
</table>

PVTV	$0.263	34.9%	|$0.263|	
NMV	$0.754	100.0%		
Derivation of Marketability Discount:				
Minority marketable value (Value of the company)				**$1.000**
Minus: non-marketable value (Shereholders value)				- **$0.754**
Discount for lack of marketability ($)				**$0.246**
Discount for lack of marketability (%)				**24.6%**

Izvor: Pratt, 2009, p. 217-218.

The presented example demonstrates the value of a non-marketable minority interest and the derived marketability discount.

The expected holding period of the shares is ten years and represents the forecast period, after which the residual value is expected to be received (i.e., the investment is expected to become marketable). The expected dividend yield of 10% represents the initial cash flow to the shareholder of $0.10 million ($1 million x 10% expected return = $0.10 million). The expected growth rate of the dividend yield (cash flow distribution to shareholders) of 5% determines the expected shareholder cash flows for each year of the projection. It is assumed that the discounting period ends at the end of each year (year 1, year 2, etc.). The expected growth in value during the holding period is 5%, resulting in a residual business value of $1.629 million ($1.05^10). In this example, there is no premium or discount at the company level. The required return during the holding period of 20% defines the present value factors applicable to each projected cash flow and the residual value.

The QMDM model inputs define the projected cash flows and the corresponding present value factors used to discount shareholder-level cash flows. The mechanism of applying present value factors to different cash flows is the same as in the standard discounted cash flow model at the company level. The indicated value of the non-marketable minority interest (V_{sh} = $0.754 million) is the sum of the present value of the cash flows ($0.491 million) and the present value of the projected residual value ($0.263 million). The corresponding marketability discount of 24.6% describes the relationship between company-level value and shareholder-level value.

Two broad categories of discounts—lack of control and lack of marketability—have a significant effect on the value of a business. Their application requires considerable professional judgment, analysis of key circumstances, and assessment of the final valuation outcome. Due to the sensitivity of the determinants involved in their calculation, estimating discounts and premiums is a serious task. However, without discounts and premiums that reflect ownership characteristics, the assessed value would not represent a reliable amount—depending on whether the valuation is viewed from the controlling or minority interest level.

3. APPLICATION OF DISCOUNTS IN THE VALUATION OF PRIVATE COMPANIES

Certain challenges in valuation arise specifically in the assessment of privately held companies. Since they are not subject to strict accounting standards and disclosure regulations, the information available for non-listed companies is much more limited in depth and historical scope. Moreover, private companies often lack crucial market inputs for risk parameter estimation, such as beta and standard deviation. The decisive factor influencing the assessed value of private firms is the purpose of the valuation (Scheibel & Klein, 2013). Unlike publicly traded companies, private firms face high transaction costs, and liquidation costs can represent a significant percentage of enterprise value. Thus, the equity value in a private business must be discounted for this potential illiquidity (Block, 2007). The illiquidity discount varies across companies and potential buyers due to the following factors:

- Liquidity of company assets – if the private firm's assets are liquid and can be sold without substantial loss of value, the illiquidity discount will be negligible;
- Financial health and cash flows – if the company has strong earnings and positive cash flows, the illiquidity discount will be lower, and vice versa;
- Possibility of becoming a public company – the greater the likelihood of listing on a capital market, the lower the illiquidity discount;
- Company size – larger firms tend to have smaller illiquidity discounts.

The value of listed companies is not publicly disclosed—only the trading price is known—and the illiquidity discount is precisely the difference between intrinsic value and price (Damodaran, 2012). Illiquidity research has been conducted on restricted stock—shares issued by public companies that are not registered with the SEC and cannot be sold on open markets for two years. Studies (e.g., Silber, 1991) showed illiquidity discounts ranging from 33.75% to 35%, covering data from 1969 to 1990. In general, illiquid investments carry a substantial discount.

A common rule of thumb for private firms suggests an illiquidity discount of 20–30% of the appraised value (Koeplin, Sarin & Shapiro, 2000). Pratt & Grabowski (2008) place it around 25%, while Block (2007) indicates a range of 20–25% for the period 1999–2006. Separately, based on U.S. studies, some authors suggest that the discount for lack of control ranges from 20–60%, though this is not strictly bounded in practice

(Shaw, 2014). American authors also note that illiquidity discounts tend to be higher for companies outside the U.S. (from their perspective).

If the appraiser chooses to adjust the illiquidity discount to reflect differences between companies, one approach is to use the discounts determined for restricted shares, while taking into account firm revenue and cash flow strength. Additionally, one may analyze bid-ask spreads for comparable listed firms within the same industry to estimate the illiquidity discount for a private business (Damodaran, 2012, p. 670).

As for control premiums, they apply when 51% or more of a private company's equity—enough to secure control—is offered for sale. Control premiums are determined similarly to those used for publicly traded firms (Pratt & Grabowski, 2008).

A private firm being sold will typically have greater value if the buyer is a publicly listed company rather than a private investor. If the buyer is diversified, market beta instead of total beta is used to calculate the cost of equity, resulting in a lower discount rate. Furthermore, the value a company may attain by entering public markets will exceed the value that a private investor might offer.

Whether and to what extent the illiquidity discount is applied depends heavily on the valuation approach and purpose. Therefore, in the valuation of private firms, crucial steps include determining the cost of equity, estimating cash flows, and calculating the illiquidity discount. Compared to publicly listed firms, the valuation purpose has a much more pronounced effect on the final assessed value of a private company.

4. EMPIRICAL RESEARCH ON THE APPLICATION OF DISCOUNTS AND PREMIUMS IN COMPANY VALUATIONS IN THE BOSNIA AND HERZEGOVINA

4.1. Research Methods and Instruments

The research methodology was developed through consultation of scientific literature and adapted to the topic and subject of the study. The research was conducted in the Bosnia and Herzegovina, analysing the state of the valuation profession and the issues of discounts and premiums in company valuations. Data was collected using a survey questionnaire based on a random sample of 78 certified and licensed appraisers in period 2015-2016. The questionnaire includes both quantitative and qualitative research characteristics. (According to the *Register of Certified Appraisers in Bosnia and Herzegovina*, there were 128 appraisers with valid licenses at the moment of research).

Most of the questions were closed-ended: direct questions, multiple-choice listing questions, and questions with intensity scale answers. Out of 100 questionnaires distributed, 78 were completed, representing a 78% response rate, which is considered a very good level of participation.

Responses to many of the questions were analysed using various scale instruments: Likert scales, as well as graphical, numerical, and descriptive scales. Given that this is a social science study involving micro-level data collection through questionnaires, the selected statistical methods came from descriptive statistics (such as proportions and graphical presentation of data) and inferential statistics, with the chi-square (χ^2) test identified as the most suitable for interpreting results.

4.2. Research Results

The analysis revealed that, in calculating premiums and discounts and determining majority and minority interests, approximately equal numbers of respondents reported valuing both controlling and minority interests (see Graph 2). It is important to emphasize a strong correlation between these practices—those who had appraised controlling interests also tended to appraise minority interests, and vice versa (see Table 2).

This relationship was statistically confirmed through the chi-square test, where:

$\chi^2_{emp} = 30.41 > \chi^2(3, 0.001) = 16.266$, indicating a statistically significant difference between the group that assessed controlling interests and the group that assessed minority interests.

Table 2:Appraisal of control and minority interest in Bosnia and Herzegovina

			Have you, in the course of your work, appraised the value of a minority interest?		**Total**
			Yes	**No**	
Have you, in the course of your work, appraised the value of a controlling interest?	**Yes**	Number	30	10	40
		%	**75.0%**	**25.0%**	**100.0%**
	No	Number	5	33	38
		%	**13.2%**	**86.8%**	**100.0%**
Total		Number	35	43	78
		%	**44.9%**	**55.1%**	**100.0%**

Hi-square test	Value	df	Significance (p)
Pearsonov χ2	30.41	3	0.00000113

Source: Author's research

Of the total number of respondents, 75% stated that they had appraised both controlling and minority interests.25% of appraisers had never appraised the value of a minority interest, but had dealt with the appraisal of controlling (i.e., majority) interests in a company.A small proportion of respondents—13.2%—had appraised a minority shareholder's equity stake without appraising a controlling interest. On the other hand, 86.8% of respondents had not appraised either a minority or a majority interest, which is a concerning finding given that the appraisal of equity value is an integral part of enterprise valuation.

The reasons for this situation, in addition to the presence of some young appraisers who have not yet conducted any appraisals independently, may also lie in the fact that a large number of appraisers only carry out partial appraisals and determine the value of specific asset categories within a company (e.g., land, a particular facility, equipment, etc.).

Appraisers who also serve as court experts are often asked to appraise only certain parts of a company's assets.

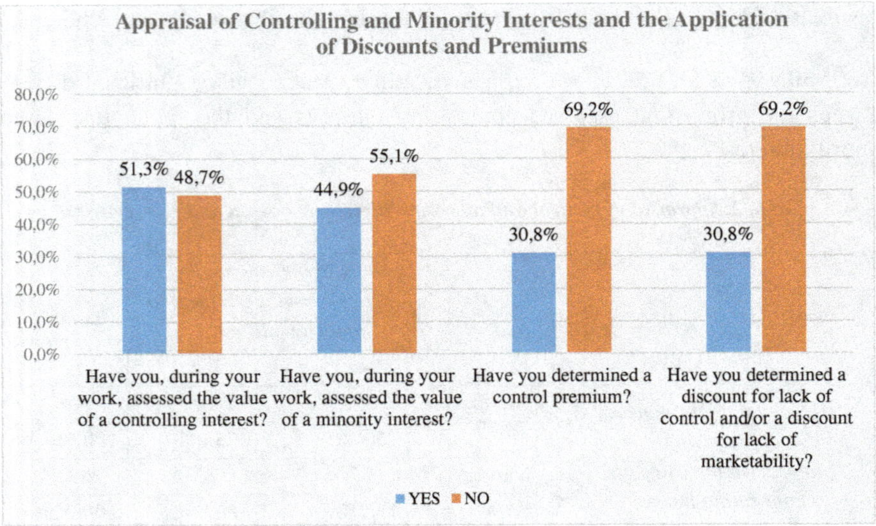

Hi-sqaure test	Value	df	Significance (p)
Pearsonov χ2	10.455	3	0.01506929
Yatesov χ2	9.059		0.02851665

Chart 2: Appraisal of Controlling and Minority Interests and the Application of Discounts and Premiums

Source: Author's research

The value of the controlling interest was assessed by 51.3% of the total number of respondents, while 44.9% gave a positive answer regarding the minority interest. As shown in the graph, the structure of valuers who determined either the control premium or the discount for lack of control / discount for lack of marketability is identical, in a 30:70 ratio. Thus, the valuers who applied premiums and discounts in their valuations (30.8%) determined both. A dependency is also expressed here ($\chi^2_{emp.}$ exceeds the critical value for significance at 5% and df=3). Specifically, those who determined the discount for lack of control / discount for lack of marketability also determined the control premium in over 70% of cases, while those who did not apply discounts in 87% of cases also did not determine the control premium. In connection with this, and in order to test the hypothesis, the following graphs are of particular interest.

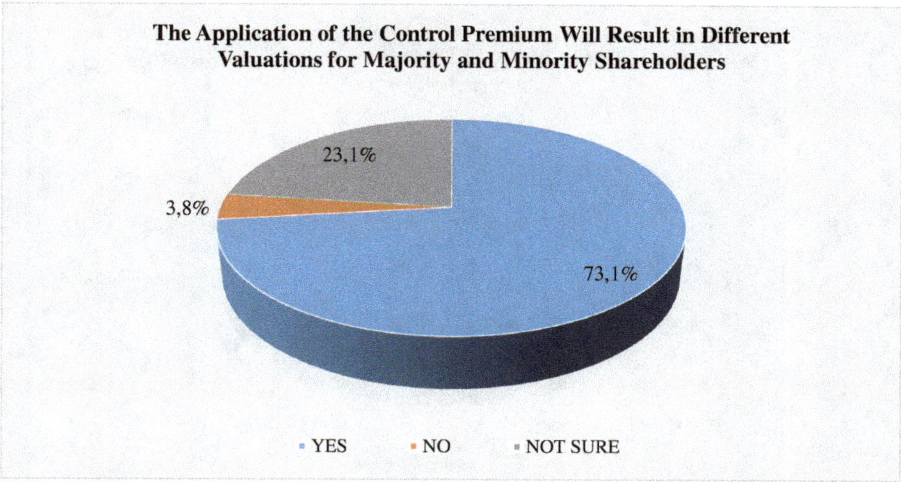

Hi-square test	Value	df	Significance (p)
Pearsonov $\chi 2$	59.769	2	0.0

Chart 3: The Impact of Control Premium on the Assessed Value of the Company

Source: Author's research

73.1% of respondents agreed with the statement that the application of a control premium leads to different assessed values for majority and minority shareholders. This is understandable, as the control premium reflects the power of control and increases the value proportionally attributed to the controlling interest.

A very small number of respondents (3.8%) disagreed with the statement, while the remaining evaluators who did not provide a positive answer were undecided. Additionally, the chi-square test, with a value significantly above the threshold (13.816) and a very low risk level of 0.1% and df=2, indicated a strong statistical difference between the number of respondents in the three groups ($p<0.001$).

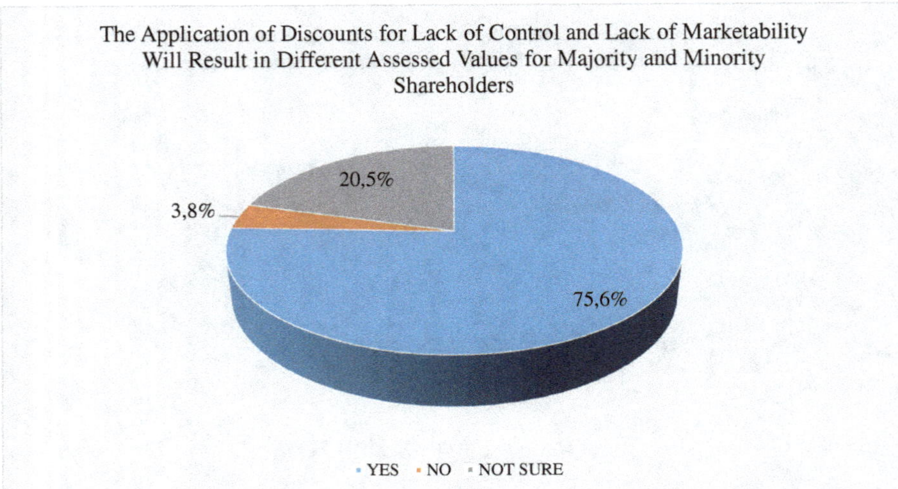

Hi-square test	Value	df	Significance (p)
Pearsonov $\chi 2$	66.077	2	0.0

Chart 4: The Impact of Discounts for Lack of Control and Lack of Marketability on the Assessed Value of a Company

Source: Author's research

A very similar situation is observed in examining the impact of discounts on the assessed value, with the percentage of appraisers who responded positively to this question increasing to 75.6%, at the expense of the undecided respondents (20.5%). As in the previous case, there is a statistically significant difference between the numbers of these three respondent groups ($p < 0.001$).

The discount for lack of marketability is applied to holdings of minority shareholders that are illiquid, and it is evident that the application of discounts for lack of marketability or lack of control will reduce the assessed value of minority interests compared to controlling interests.

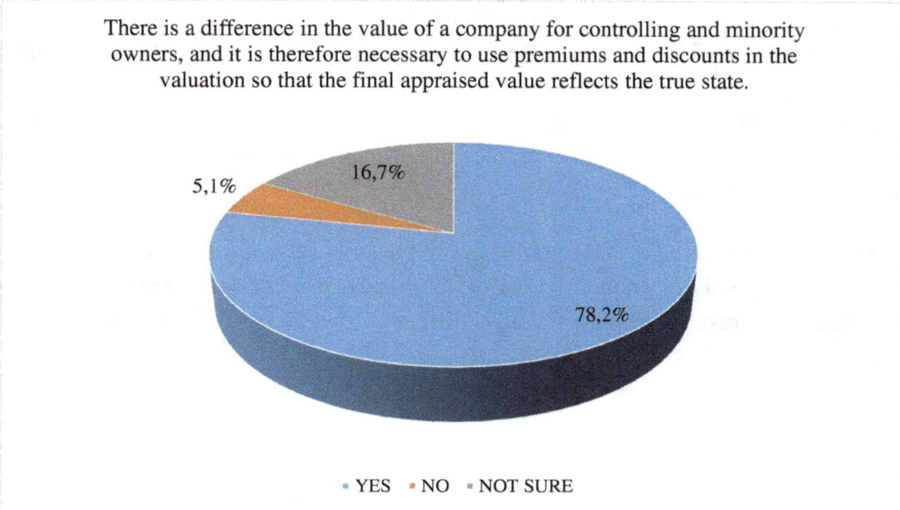

Hi-square test	Value	df	Significance (p)
Pearsonov χ2	72.231	2	0.0

Chart 5: The Importance of Discounts and Premiums in Determining Controlling and Minority Interests

Source: Author's research

Only 5% of respondents believe that there is no difference in company value between controlling and minority owners, and therefore that it is not necessary to apply premiums and discounts for the valuation to reflect the true state. A total of 16.7% of respondents were unsure how to answer this question, while the vast majority (78.2%) agreed with the statement. As with the previous two questions, the statistical difference between the three groups of appraisers is significant, with a 0.1% risk of error (χ^2emp. > $\chi^2(2, 0.001)$).

It is evident that in our country, the valuation profession still harbours doubts and open questions regarding the application of discounts and premiums, indicating a need to enhance knowledge in this area of valuation.

From the above, it is clear that most respondents are familiar with and estimate the value of the controlling interest, while a smaller percentage determine the minority interest value. The minority interest, when adjusted by applying discounts, is determined in 30.8% of cases, while 14.1% of appraisers determine minority interest value in the same way as the controlling interest.

As capital markets strengthen over time and more citizens become involved in shareholder ownership, the need to determine the value of minority interests will undoubtedly grow. Therefore, education in this area of valuation is necessary, as is emphasizing the importance and necessity of applying appropriate discounts. Even now, there is demand for the valuation of minority shareholders' equity in court cases dealing with this issue.

The results confirm the initial hypothesis, as they clearly indicate that—according to the surveyed appraisers (more than 70% of them)—the application of control premiums and discounts results in significantly different valuations for controlling versus minority shareholders.

CONCLUSION

The value of a company and the application of discounts are considered from two perspectives: that of the *majority owner (discounts at the enterprise level)* and that of *minority shareholders (discounts at the shareholder level). Enterprise-level discounts* apply to the overall value and affect all shareholders, being applied to the controlling interest, whereas *shareholder-level discounts* (such as discounts for lack of control and discounts for lack of marketability) are relevant to specific groups, such as minority shareholders or shareholders without voting rights.

Accordingly, methods for determining the value of controlling interests include all methods within the income, market, and cost approaches, while methods for minority interest valuation may be direct or indirect. Indirect methods involve subtracting the discount for lack of control and the discount for lack of marketability from the value of the controlling interest.

When valuing private companies, due to the absence of market data, higher transaction costs, and reduced liquidity, a liquidity discount is applied. This discount reflects the difference between the estimated value and the price at which a private company can be bought or sold, and it is typically significant in illiquid investments. Shareholder-level discounts, such as those for lack of control and lack of marketability, can materially affect the assessed value of a company.

This study established a correlation between the valuation of controlling and minority interests, indicating that in cases where control premiums were determined, discounts were also applied—and vice versa. The findings reveal that most practitioners assess controlling interests, while minority interest valuations are less frequently applied in practice. The use of control premiums, along with the relevant shareholder-level discounts, results in different valuation outcomes for majority and minority shareholders. To ensure the final appraised value accurately reflects ownership structure, it is necessary to apply appropriate discounts and premiums, thus confirming the central hypothesis of the study.

In conclusion, valuation practice in the Bosnia and Herzegovina still faces ambiguities and unresolved issues regarding the use of discounts and premiums. As the capital market strengthens over time and as more citizens engage in shareholder ownership, the need for minority interest valuations will undoubtedly increase. This highlights the importance of education and awareness in this area, especially given the current demand for minority equity valuations in court proceedings. The application of discounts and premiums requires significant professional judgment, contextual analysis, and a clear assessment of the likely valuation outcome. Given the sensitivity of the factors involved, calculating these adjustments is a complex and demanding task. However, without incorporating ownership-specific discounts and premiums, the resulting value cannot be deemed reliable, whether viewed from a controlling or minority ownership perspective.

REFERENCES

American Institute of Certified Public Accountants (AICPA). (2012). *International Glossary of Business Valuation Terms. Statement on Standards for Valuation Services No. 1*. AICPA. http://www.aicpa.org/InterestAreas/ForensicAndValuation/Resources/Standards/downloadabledocuments/international_glossary_of_bv_terms.pdf

American Society of Appraisers (ASA). (2009). *ASA Business Valuation Standards*. ASA.http://www.appraisers.org/docs/defaultsource/discipline_bv/bvstandards.pdf?sfvrsn=0

Block, S. (2007). The Liquidity Discount in Valuing Privately Owned Companies. *Journal of Applied Finance*, *17*(2), 33-40.

Damodaran, A. (2012). *Investment Valuation: Tools and Techniques for Determining the Value of Any Asset.* 3rd Ed. John Wiley and Sons.

DiMattia, R.D. (2008). Controlling Interests – Discount for Lack of Marketability: the Empirical Evidence. *CPA Expert.* Summer, 2008. http://www.corporatevaluepartners.com/news/art_081208.pdf.

Garner, B. A. (ed.). (2014). *Black's Law Dictionary*. 10th Ed. New York: Thompson West.

Koeplin, J., Sarin, A. & Shapiro, A. (2000). The Private Company Discount. *Journal of Applied Corporate Finance*, *12*(4), 94-101. https://doi.org/10.1111/j.1745-6622.2000.tb00022.x

Mikerević, D. (2009). *Principi i praksa procjene vrijednosti preduzeća*. Finrar, Banja Luka.

Pratt, S. (2009). *Business Valuation: Discounts and Premiums*. John Wiley and Sons.

Pratt, S., & Grabowski, R. J. (2008). *Cost of Capital: Estimation and Applications. 3rd Ed.* John Wiley and Sons.

Scheibel, M. & Klein, C. (2013). What Influences the Discount Applied to the Valuation for Controlling Interests in Private Companies? (An Analysis Based on the Acquisition Approach for Comparable Transactions of European Private and Public Target Companies). *Journal of Business Valuation and Economic Loss Analysis*, *8*(1),1-25.

Silber, W. L. (1991). Discounts on Restricted Stock: The Impact of Illiquidity on Stock Prices. *Financial Analysts Journal*, *47*(4), 60-64.

Shaw, J. (2014). *Liquidity Discounts for Valuations of Closely Held Businesses*. Grant Thornton. http://www.grant-thornton.co.uk/Global/Publication_pdf/liquidity-discounts-for-valuations-of-closely-held-businesses.pdf.

V [*]VALUATION OF START-UP COMPANIES UNDER CONDITIONS OF UNCERTAINTY

Abstract

The valuation of a company is a complex and demanding process that requires a wide range of inputs, which is particularly pronounced in the case of valuing early-stage companies. Many critical pieces of information—such as revenues, net cash flows, financial statements, comparable company data, stock price movements, and more - are typically unavailable when valuing start-up companies. Start-ups are characterized by the following features: a lack or significant limitation of historical data, illiquid investments, low revenues, losses in operations, reliance on private capital, and a high failure rate in the first years of existence. The application of traditional valuation methods is often limited in these cases, especially under uncertainty, and requires adaptation and modification. Contemporary literature therefore proposes alternative valuation approaches for early-stage businesses. These alternative methods focus on future projections instead of historical data, use scenario-based modeling, and analyze the characteristics and business models specific to the company being valued. Valuation methods for early-stage companies must consider these characteristics, reduce the level of uncertainty, ensure a more reliable valuation, and ultimately arrive at a relevant and dependable estimate of company value.

Keywords: *valuation, valuation methods, traditional valuation methods, alternative valuation methods, start-up companies.*

---

[*] *Originally published in 2024 in the Proceedings of the XVIII International Congress of the Accounting and Auditing Profession of Republic of Srpska (Bosnia and Herzegovina), Banja Vrućica, pp. 237–258. Reused here with permission from the publisher.*

INTRODUCTION

The valuation of a start-up company is defined as the process of determining how much a start-up and its assets are worth at a given point in time, with the most commonly sought value being fair market value. A start-up is generally considered to be a company with a maximum of 150 employees, operating independently, and active for less than ten years within a limited geographic area (Davila & Foster, 2005). Another definition sets three criteria for a start-up: it is younger than ten years, possesses highly innovative technologies or business models, and aims for significant growth in revenue and employment (Kollmann et al., 2016). The broadest and most widely accepted definition is that a start-up is: "a new business that has been started from scratch" (Kolvereid & Isaksen, 2006).

Valuing start-ups is unique in many ways and requires the analysis of various elements, such as capital structure, projected cash flows, earnings estimates, and other financial information. Many of these data are simply not available in early-stage companies, including historical performance, data on investments, revenues and profits, net cash flows, stock price movements (in case of corporations), comparable company benchmarks, and other market information.

Key factors that define a start-up and influence its valuation include (Walton, 2024a):

- *Company age or maturity*, which significantly impacts the associated risks and the amount and type of data available for valuation. Early-stage businesses are riskier and have fewer historical data points, while more mature start-ups offer more operational history and potentially more stable revenues. Start-ups are usually categorized into four stages (Eqvista, 2024):
    - Seed Stage: the business is still an idea with no substantial assets and generates little to no revenue;
    - Series A: the company has developed a prototype and started generating some revenue from sales;
    - Series B: the business has demonstrated viability and seeks to scale profitability based on its business model;
    - Series C: the business is generating significant revenue and may be preparing for acquisition or an IPO.
- *Market size potential*, which indicates the upper limit of the company's earning capacity. Larger markets provide greater growth potential and positively impact the start-up's estimated value.

- *Product development stage* (concept, prototype, fully developed product, etc.), which correlates with risk level. The more advanced the product, the lower the risk and the higher the company's valuation due to stronger business viability signals.
- *A strong and experienced management team* can significantly increase a start-up's value. Managerial experience generally reduces the likelihood of failure and increases the probability of profitable operations.
- *Historical growth and future growth* potential are critical valuation factors, as rapid growth in revenue, user base, or market share leads to a higher estimated company value.

Start-ups play a crucial role in any economy, driving economic value, technological innovation, and job creation. Therefore, identifying and applying appropriate valuation methods is essential to ensure that the resulting valuation is both relevant and reliable.

Given the specific nature of start-ups, academic literature discusses both traditional and alternative valuation methods suited to these companies. Although there is no consensus on a single best method—since each has its advantages, limitations, and potential for refinement—it is recommended to use multiple valuation approaches to arrive at the most representative and dependable value for a start-up company.

1. PREVIOUS RESEARCH

Methods for valuing newly established companies can be divided into traditional and alternative approaches. Traditional methods include the income, market, and cost approaches. Another way to classify valuation methods for start-ups is into: quantitative methods based on scientific tools that rely on measurable data and calculations, and qualitative methods that employ a subjective approach to valuation. Traditional methods are mostly quantitative, whereas alternative methods may be either quantitative or qualitative.

One group of theorists argues that traditional methods are not suitable for valuing start-ups due to the unavailability of required inputs, historical data, and the financial and market information necessary for conducting the valuation process (Dehghan-Eshratabad & Albadvi, 2018; Dusatkova & Zinecker, 2016). Regarding income methods, the Discounted Cash Flow (DCF) method may be used to estimate the value of high-growth companies that have not yet reached operational maturity (IVSC, 2012; Laitinen, 2019). Challenges in applying the DCF method to start-ups include: high uncertainty of future cash flows (Shestakov, 2015), the significant role of terminal value in valuing start-ups (Reis & Augusto, 2013), difficulties in determining terminal value due to unresolved questions about if, when, and how the company will grow (Damodaran, 2016), and the estimation of the discount rate using the CAPM model (Hoseini & Moradi Esfanjani, 2019). CAPM can be problematic for determining the discount rate of a start-up since it relies on sector characteristics, company history, and homogenous market risk. In early-stage companies, it is impossible to extrapolate past returns, beta is difficult to determine, and total company risk is primarily firm-specific rather than market-based (Montani, Gervasio & Pulcini, 2020).

The market approach is also difficult to apply to start-ups. This is because the multiples used in the comparable companies and precedent transactions methods are based on profit or revenue, which are often negative in new ventures. Additionally, it is very difficult to find comparable market data, as each start-up typically has unique characteristics (Montani, Gervasio & Pulcini, 2020). Market data is generally available for mature companies, not for early-stage ventures (Damodaran, 2009).

The cost approach is generally considered the least suitable for valuing start-ups. Its limitations stem from its inherent characteristics: cost methods are static, asset-based, and do not take into account future developments or future operations (De Olivera & Zotes, 2018). An exception is the use of cost methods for start-ups in the very earliest (embryonic) stage of development, when reliable cash flow projections cannot be made, and the company's value may roughly equal the amount of initial invested capital (Beaton, 2010). The book value method stands out as particularly useful in valuing newly established companies (Rotich, 2024). The Real Option Method (Black & Scholes, 1973; Copeland, Koller & Murrin, 2000; Frykman & Tolleryd, 2012) is also frequently applied in valuing early-stage companies.

In light of the above, numerous debates and studies have emerged in academic circles, resulting in alternative valuation methods for start-ups. Given the lack of key financial and historical data, non-financial information is particularly important for valuing newly established companies (Köhn, 2018). Many valuation methods for start-ups are based precisely on such non-financial information (Miloud et al., 2012). Some of the most commonly used alternative methods for valuing start-ups include:

Quantitative Methods:

- *First Chicago Method* – FCM (Achleitner & Lutz, 2005; Babiarz, 2016);
- *Venture Capital Method* – VCM (Damodaran, 2009; Keeley, Punjabi & Turki, 1996; Sahlman & Scherlis, 1987);
- *Modified DCF Method* (Damodaran, 2009; Festel, Wuermseher & Cattaneo, 2013; Koller, Goedhart & Wessels, 2020).

Qualitative Methods:

- *Berkus Method* (Berkus, 2012, 2016; Amis & Stevenson, 2001);
- *Scorecard Method* (Payne, 2011a; Rose, 2014);
- *Risk Factor Summation Method* (Karius, 2016; Payne, 2011b; Babu, Arikutaram & Mathews, 2023).

Empirical models for valuing start-ups have been developed by investors to assess their own investments. These include:

- *Rule of Thirds* (Mothersill et al., 2009);
- *Replacement Method and the Value-Based Balance Sheet* (Kallir & Agmon, 2015);
- *Berkus Method;*
- *Scorecard Method;*
- *Risk Factor Summation Method* already mentioned.

Thus, in addition to the traditional methods widely used for valuing start-ups, a range of alternative methods also exists. The choice of method, or combination of methods, will depend on the characteristics and specificities of the particular company, its industry, the market in which it operates, the availability of financial and market data, its current performance, and the stage of development in which the start-up is located.

2. TRADITIONAL METHODS FOR VALUING START-UP COMPANIES

Traditional valuation methods are well-known and widely accepted approaches that have been used for decades to assess the value of companies, capital, and assets. These methods are typically classified into the income, market, and cost approaches. When valuing a company that is in a later stage of development, possesses historical data, and has access to financial and market information—but can still be considered a start-up—traditional methods are appropriate for application.

The four most commonly used traditional methods for valuing newly established companies are: the Discounted Cash Flow (DCF) method, the Comparable Companies method, the Precedent Transactions method, and the Real Options method.

2.1. Discounted Cash Flow (DCF) Method

The DCF method is the most widely used valuation method in practice, both for start-ups and for companies in general. As the name suggests, this method estimates a company's value by discounting its future cash flows to present value using an appropriate discount rate. The DCF method is suitable for start-ups that have stable cash flows and certain available financial data—i.e., companies that are not in the earliest stage of development. The valuation process is the same as for any other company: the present value of expected cash flows is calculated by discounting annual projected cash flows using a discount rate that reflects the cost of capital.

2.2. Comparable Companies Method

Market-based methods (the Comparable Companies and Precedent Transactions methods) value a company by comparing it to similar firms for which financial data is publicly available. The essence of both methods lies in developing valuation multiples based on share prices of the company being assessed and comparable companies traded on capital markets (Serdar Raković, 2020). The most commonly used financial multiples in the Comparable Companies method for estimating the market value of start-ups are (Damodaran, 2002):

- Price-to-Earnings (P/E),
- Price-to-Sales (P/S),
- Enterprise Value-to-EBITDA (EV/EBITDA), and
- Price-to-Book Value (P/B)

Thus:

Company value = Financial indicator × Average industry multiple

When applied to start-ups, the process typically includes the following steps:

1) Identifying and selecting appropriate comparable companies;
2) Collecting financial data of the comparables;
3) Defining financial parameters and multiples to be used in the valuation;
4) Calculating the average multiple;
5) Estimating market value.

Example 1 *(based on Walton, 2024b):* We are estimating the value of start-up company X in the field of artificial intelligence in healthcare.

1) **Identify comparable start-ups**: Start-ups A, B, and C operating in the same industry and at similar development stages.
2) **Collect financial data:**

   Start-up A: 100,000 users; company value: BAM 15 million

   Start-up B: 80,000 users; company value: BAM 10 million

   Start-up C: 120,000 users; company value: BAM 20 million

3) Define financial parameters and calculate multiples:

   Multiple for the company = estimated value / number of customers

   A: 15 million / 100,000 = BAM 150 per user

   B: 10 million / 80,000 = BAM 125 per user

   C: 20 million / 120,000 = BAM 166.67 per user

4) Calculate the average industry multiple:

Average industry multiple = (Multiple for Company A + Multiple for Company B + Multiple for Company C) / number of comparable companies

Average industry multiple = (150 + 125 + 166.67) / 3 ≈ BAM 147.22 per user

5) Adjustment for Specific Characteristics of the Valued Company and Estimation of Market Value

If the technology of the valued company is more advanced (which could increase customer engagement or retention), the average multiplier can be adjusted. In this example, we adjust the average multiplier from 147.22 to 150 BAM per customer due to the advanced technology of company X.

Adjusted company value = Adjusted multiplier × customer base

Adjusted value of company X = 150 BAM per customer × 90,000 customers = 13.5 million BAM

The final estimated value is 13.5 million BAM after adjusting for the unique technology and market position of the valued company X.

The comparable companies method is effective for start-up companies operating in industry sectors where many companies are listed on capital markets, providing relevant data for comparison. The final estimated value of BAM 13.5 million reflects the company's advanced technology and unique market position.

The Comparable Companies method is efficient for start-ups operating in industries with many listed firms, where relevant data is available for comparison.

2.3. Precedent Transactions Method

The Precedent Transactions method values a company by analyzing prices paid for similar companies in past acquisition deals. It considers the premiums that buyers were historically willing to pay for companies within the same industry (Walton, 2024a). This method involves identifying relevant transactions from recent years, determining the range of valuation multiples, and applying those multiples to the company being assessed.

Example 2: Assume we are valuing Company A in the service sector. Similar companies in the same industry were acquired at an average multiple of 4× revenue. The company being valued has sales revenue of 10 million BAM.

Thus, the value of company A = 4 × 10 million BAM = 40 million BAM.

This method is particularly effective in industry sectors where acquisitions are common and there is sufficient evidence of past sales and transactions.

2.4. Real Option Valuation Method

The Real Option Pricing Model (ROM) is theoretically based on the binomial and Black-Scholes models (Copeland, Koller & Murrin, 2000). The value of equity in companies can be viewed as a call option. The option is in the hands of the shareholders who may choose to liquidate the company and claim the difference between the value of the company and the amount of debt. Given their limited liability, the equity retains value even when the value of the assets is lower than the unpaid debt due to the time premium of the option. The obligations of investors -shareholders when companies are listed on capital markets are limited to their ownership share, and the ability to liquidate the company with limited shareholder liability is a feature of a call option.

Real options imply the application of financial option pricing theory to real (physical) assets. Therefore, ROM can capture the management's ability and flexibility to adapt and revise future decisions in response to unexpected market developments (Wardani & Fujiwara, 2018).

Valuation based on real options assesses the flexibility to change strategy in response to future events. The valuation involves complex financial modeling, using option pricing techniques.

Example 3 (according to Damodaran, 2002): We need to assess the value of equity in the newly established company B. The company has more debt than equity. The financial parameters for company B are as follows:

- Value of underlying asset = S = Value of the company = $50 million
- Value of debt = $80 million
- Option strike price = K = nominal value of the debt = $80 million
- Option duration = t = maturity of a zero-coupon bond = 10 years
- Standard deviation of the asset value = 40%

- Variance of the underlying asset = ρ^2 = variance in the company's value = 0.16
- Risk-free rate r = yield on government bonds with the same maturity as the option = 10%

We apply the real option model, and the Black-Scholes model gives:

D1 = 1.0515	N(d1) = 0.8534
D2 = −0.2135	N(d2) = 0.4155

$$\text{Equity value as an option} = 50 \times (0.8534) - 80\text{exp}^{(-0.10)(10)}(0.4155) = \$30.44 \text{ million}$$

The option value is the value of equity = $30.44 million

The value of outstanding debt = $50 million – $30.44 million = $19.56 million

Equity in the company has value due to the characteristics of the option inherent in the equity itself.

The real options method is recommended for valuing start-up companies, especially in highly volatile industries with uncertain future conditions, for companies operating with high risk, and for valuing enterprises or projects involving significant investments in innovative technologies, real estate development, or natural resources.

3. ALTERNATIVE METHODS FOR VALUING START-UP COMPANIES

Alternative methods are grouped into quantitative and qualitative, and will be presented in the following sections according to this classification.

3.1 Quantitative Methods for Valuing Start-Up Companies

3.1.1. Venture Capital Method

The Venture Capital Method (VCM) is used for valuing start-up companies in the capital-raising phase, in order to determine the value of the company before and after the new capital is raised. It is based on the DCF method and was developed by Sahlman & Scherlis (1987). The method is particularly useful in determining the percentage of ownership in the capital of new and existing equity holders. It relies on the present value of discounted future cash flows according to the most likely scenario, under the assumption of a limited time horizon and using a discount rate that reflects the high risk of the investment. Special attention is paid to business risk when applying this valuation method.

The valuation process using the Venture Capital Method consists of three steps (Montani, Gervasio & Pulcini, 2020):

1) Estimate expected cash flows over a projection period of 2 to 5 years (Damodaran, 2009). The projection period corresponds to the expected time until company exit or initial public offering (IPO). The terminal value at the end of the projection period is calculated by multiplying the expected cash flows by a capital multiplier (usually a P/E ratio, defined based on the market prices of comparable companies).
2) The terminal value of the company is assessed at the so-called exit point (typically estimated using market-based methods) and discounted to present value using a very high discount rate, representing the required return of the venture capital investor (ROI).
3) Based on the invested venture capital, the ownership share of each capital owner is determined:

$$NPV_{after\ raising\ capital} = NPV_{before\ raising\ capital} \times Invested\ amount\ (I_{0,vc})$$

The ownership stake belonging to the investor who contributed capital is obtained by dividing the amount of capital invested by the value of the company after the capital injection.

Value after raising capital (Post-Money) = Exit value / Expected ROI

Value before capital raising (Pre-Money) = Value after raising capital (Post-Money) - Investment amount

Example 4 (according to Walton, 2024a): We are estimating the value of company C using the venture capital method.

The exit value of the company is $100 million.

The expected ROI is 10x.

The investment amount is $5 million.

Value after raising capital (Post-Money) = $100 million / 10 = $10 million

Value before capital raising (Pre-Money) = $10 million – $5 miliona = $5 milliona

Investor Ownership Share (for investor who invested capital) = $5 million /$10 million = 50%

The venture capital method is useful for start-up companies that are not yet generating high revenues, anticipate significant growth, and plan acquisitions or an exit to capital markets through an initial public offering (IPO) within a foreseeable timeframe.

Some of the method's drawbacks include the inability to consider multiple scenarios and the incorporation of high risk into a discount rate that remains constant throughout the company's life cycle, which is not a realistic assumption (Damodaran, 2009).

3.1.2. The First Chicago Method (FCM)

The First Chicago Method (FCM) combines elements of income-based and market-based valuation methods. It is named after the first fund that applied it for valuation purposes—the Chicago Corporation Fund. The First Chicago Method is a modification of the venture capital method and includes the use of a lower discount rate. In this method, terminal value is replaced by the net present value of the investment, determined as the average value of the startup under different scenarios: optimistic, most likely, and pessimistic. FCM considers all three scenarios and assigns a probability of realization to each. The method consists of three stages (Montani, Gervasio & Pulcini, 2020):

1) All three scenarios are defined, and financial forecasts are prepared for each;
2) The exit value of the business in each scenario is determined using valuation multiples (comparable transactions based on industry type, geographic location, and stage in the company's life cycle). This constitutes the terminal value at the time of sale;
3) The value of the startup is estimated as the sum of the net present values of each scenario (terminal value plus expected cash flows up to the planned exit), weighted by the probability of each scenario occurring.

$$PV_i = \sum_{t=1}^{h} \frac{CF_t^i}{(1+r)^t} + \frac{TV_i}{(1+r)^h} \Rightarrow PV = \sum_{i=1}^{3} p_i \times PV_i$$

Where:

i = scenario index

h = time until exit

p = probability of each scenario occurring

r = discount rate

PV = present value

CF = cash flows during period t

TV = terminal value

Example 5: Determining the value of a start-up company D using the First Chicago Method (FCM)

The company's value was assessed using three scenarios, each assigned a probability of occurrence:

- Optimistic scenario: $10 million (30% probability)
- Most likely (realistic) scenario: $5 million (50% probability)
- Pessimistic scenario: $1 million (20% probability)

Expected value of the start-up company D = ($10 million × 0.3) + ($5 million × 0.5) + ($1 million × 0.2) = $3 million + $2.5 million + $0.2 million = $5.7 million

Since the First Chicago Method considers multiple scenarios and identifies risks specific to start-ups, it results in a more realistic valuation compared to the Venture Capital Method. However, FCM does not account for potential changes in circumstances and is best suited for start-up companies that are already generating revenue (Demyanova, 2018).

3.1.3. The Cost-to-Duplicate Method

The Cost-to-Duplicate Method values a start-up company based on the cost of replacing its assets. It is most similar to cost approach methods. The company's value is determined as the fair market value of its tangible assets; however, this may also include software development costs and research and development (R&D) expenses.

The cost-to-duplicate method does not take into account the company's future sales potential or growth, nor does it include intangible assets such as brand value, goodwill, or intellectual property. Investors who apply this method are generally not willing to invest more than the market value of the company.

The value of a start-up is determined as follows (Walton, 2024a):

Estimated value of the start-up = Total R&D costs + technology development costs + replacement cost of tangible assets + prototype/initial production costs

Example 6: We are valuing company E using the cost-to-duplicate method. The company's data are as follows:

- R&D: $1 million
- Technology development: $2 million
- Tangible assets: $3 million
- Product prototype: $0.5 million

Total duplication cost (i.e., company value) = $1 million + $2 million + $3 million + $0.5 million = $6.5 million

This method is suitable for risk-averse investors because it is highly objective—based on actual replacement cost data. It is used in the early stages of start-up development when there is insufficient revenue but significant investment in development. As with other methods, it is recommended to combine this method with another valuation method to ensure a more reliable estimate.

3.1.4. Modified DCF Method

Given the irreplaceability of the DCF method, many authors argue that - with appropriate adjustments - it can be highly suitable for valuing start-up companies (Festel, Wuermseher & Cattaneo, 2013; Koller, Goedhart & Wessels, 2020). Damodaran developed his own DCF model specifically for valuing early-stage companies, with numerous modifications that take into account the specific characteristics of the business (Damodaran, 2009).

When estimating the value of cash flows, Damodaran overcomes the lack of historical data by applying two alternative methodologies: top-down and bottom-up approaches. These are based on analyzing the (albeit uncertain) future rather than the past.

The **top-down approach** involves analyzing the potential market, estimating the company's market share, operating margins, investment requirements for growth, tax effects, and conducting consistency checks.

The **bottom-up approach** is simpler and resembles budgeting, where results depend on accurate forecasting of revenues and expected cash flows.

When projecting the **discount rate**, the model starts with the unlevered industry beta, then calculates the specific company's levered beta, and finally derives the beta for venture capital.

For estimating **terminal value**, Damodaran (2009) proposes choosing one of the following methods, depending on the characteristics of the start-up:

- Value the company as a growing firm under the assumption of constant cash flow growth.
- Assume a specific growth period for cash flows and estimate the present value of those cash flows.
- Value the company under the assumption that it will be liquidated at the end of the projection period, with the accumulated asset value representing the terminal value.

The choice among these three approaches depends on the nature of the company being valued.

Another factor introduced in the modified DCF method is the adjustment for the company's survival probability. In the first stage, the company is valued assuming it continues operating. In the second stage, the possibility of failure is introduced. Finally, the start-up's value is calculated as the present value of the weighted average of these two scenarios (growth scenario and default scenario).

The modified DCF method is suitable for valuing start-ups that face difficulties in raising capital or whose success depends heavily on one or a few key individuals.

3.2. Qualitative Methods for Valuing Start-Up Companies

These methods rely more on judgment and evaluation, such as assessing the expertise of the management team, market potential, and innovative business models, rather than solely on concrete figures and financial data, which are often lacking in many start-up companies. Early-stage ventures are characterized by high sustainability risks and uncertain futures, so valuations are frequently conducted through analysis of these determinants and the application of qualitative methods.

3.2.1. The Berkus Method

The Berkus Method (BM) is a qualitative valuation method that assigns a monetary value to key qualitative determinants of a start-up. The method was introduced by Dave Berkus in 1996 and is named after him. The latest version of the Berkus Method identifies five common risk factors, and each factor is assigned a financial value, ranging from $0 to $500,000.

The risk factors are valued as follows (Berkus, 2016):

- Business Idea (basic value);
- Technology / Prototype (reducing technological risk);
- Quality Management Team (reducing execution risk);
- Strategic Relationships (reducing market risk);
- Product Rollout or Sales (reducing production risk).

After assigning up to $500,000 to each of these five key elements, the total assigned values are summed to determine the estimated pre-money valuation of the start-up. The cap of $500,000 per risk factor means that the maximum estimated valuation under the Berkus Method is $2.5 million.

Example 7: Let us assume that for the start-up company F, the following values are assigned to each risk factor:

Table 1: Valuation of a Start-Up Using the Berkus Method

	Risk factors	**Amount in $**
1.	Business idea	300.000
2.	Tehnology	400.000
3.	Quality management team	450.000
4.	Strategic relationships	350.000
5.	Product rollout or sales	250.000
6.	**Total value of the company (sum from 1 to 5)**	**1.750.000**

Izvor: Walton, 2024a

The total value of company F according to the Berkus Method is $1,750,000.

The Berkus Method has undergone several versions. The latest version of the method is more flexible and even allows for individual factors to be assigned more than $500,000 in total, if such values are typical for a given industry sector (Montani, Gervasio & Pulcini, 2020).

The method is widely used by angel investors. The Berkus Method (BM) is used to value companies in the early stages of development, when there is insufficient financial information and before generating revenue, and when the assumption is that the company will reach significant revenue of at least $20 million in the future (typically within five years) (Berkus, 2012). It is considered highly suitable when combined with the Venture Capital Method (Kowlessar, 2016).

The limitations of the method lie in the cap on the estimated value, its focus on only five factors, and the high degree of subjectivity in value assessment.

3.2.2. Scorecard Method

The Scorecard Method (SM) is an innovative valuation approach that assesses the value of a start-up by comparing it to other young companies in the same sector or region, and by weighing various aspects of its value. The method was developed by investor Bill Payne. Only companies in the same life cycle stage are used as comparables (Payne, 2011a).

The valuation process using the Scorecard Method consists of the following steps:

1) **Identify the average value of comparable companies** in the industry or geographic region (pre-money) as the base value;
2) **Identify key factors and assign weightings** based on their importance:

- Strength of the management team (0–30%);
- Market opportunity (0–25%);
- Product/Technology (0–15%);
- Competitive environment (0–10%);
- Marketing/Sales channels/Partnerships (0–10%);
- Need for additional investment (0–5%);
- Other factors (0–5%).

3) **Compare the start-up being evaluated** with the average using the factors listed above;
4) **Assign a score (%)** to each factor based on performance relative to the average (a specific feature of this method is that scores may exceed 100% if the company is above average);
5) **Multiply** the weight of each factor by its score to calculate the factor multipliers;
6) **Sum the factor multipliers** to determine the total adjustment factor;

7) **Multiply the total adjustment factor by the average pre-money valuation**: the estimated value of the start-up is the product of the summed factor multipliers and the average valuation.

Example 8: The average pre-money value is $2 million. We are evaluating company G using the Scorecard Method. The weights, scores, and factor multipliers are as follows:

Table 2: ***Valuation of a Start-Up Using the Scorecard Method***

	Factors	**Ponder (%) (1)**	**Result (2)**	**Factors multiplicators (3) = (1) x (2)**
1.	Management team	30	120	0.30 x 1.20 = 0.36
2.	Level of market opportunity	25	110	0.25 x 1.10 = 0.275
3.	Product/tehnology	15	100	0.15 x 1.00 =0.15
4.	Competitive environment	10	90	0.10 x 0.90 =0.09
5.	Marketing/Sales channels/Partnerships	10	80	0.10 x 0.80 =0.08
6.	Need for additional investment	5	100	0.05 x 1.00 = 0.05
7.	Other factors	5	100	0.05 x 1.00 = 0.05
8.	Total adjustment factor (sum of column 3)			1.0554
9.	Adjusted value of company ($2 million x 1.0554)			**$2.11 million**

Izvor: Walton, 2024a

Similar to the Berkus Method, the Scorecard Method focuses on key aspects in the valuation of a start-up (Rose, 2014). The Scorecard Method helps angel investors evaluate start-up companies before they generate revenue. It has shown the greatest usefulness for companies that demonstrate initial market appeal but lack long-term financial data. Like other methods, this approach has certain limitations, such as the considerable subjectivity involved in assigning weights to the various factors that determine the final valuation.

3.2.3. Risk Factor Summation Method

The Risk Factor Summation Method, like the previous two qualitative methods (BM and SM), uses a list of factors to evaluate start-up companies in the pre-revenue stage. The method was developed by investors from Ohio (USA) (Montani, Gervasio & Pulcini, 2020). The value of the company is determined by adding or subtracting from a base value according to the perceived business risks.

The first step is to identify comparable young companies in the same industry. After that, a list of risks associated with the company is compiled. The steps in the Risk Factor Summation Method are as follows (Walton, 2024a):

1) **Identify comparable companies** (same industry, location, and stage of the business life cycle);
2) **Identify relevant risk factors**, such as:

- Management risk;
- Stage of the business;
- Legislative/political risk;
- Production risk;
- Sales and marketing risk;
- Financial/funding risk;
- Competitive risk;
- Technological risk;
- Litigation risk;
- International risk;
- Reputational risk;
- Exit value risk.

3) **Assess each risk** and assign it a rating from -2 to +2, depending on the level of risk adjustment required for the company being evaluated, compared to the average value of comparable companies.

Table 3: Risk Factor Summation and Adjustment of the Sector's Average Value

Rating	Meaning	Adjustment to the average estimated pre-money value
2	Very positive for business growth and ideal exit strategy	+ $500.000
1	Positive	+ $250.000
0	Neutral	No correction
-1	Negative	- $500.000
-2	Very negative for business growth and ideal exit strategy	- $250.000

Izvor: Montani, Gervasio & Pulcini, 2020

4) **Adjust the** average value by $250,000 for each +1 result and by $500,000 for each +2 result. For negative ratings, the same amounts are subtracted from the average value.

5) **The adjusted value of the company is calculated** as follows (Kowlessar, 2016):

Value of the start-up (pre-money valuation) = Average estimated pre-money value for the sector ± total adjustment

Example 9: Let us assume that the average estimated value of comparable companies in the sector before capital acquisition is 5 million US dollars. The following ratings have been assigned to the risk factors:

Table 4: Application of the Risk Factor Summation Method

	Risk factors	Total adjustment in $
1.	Management Risk	+250.000
2.	Stage of Business	+ 0
3.	Legislative/Political Risk	– 250.000
4.	Production Risk	+ 500.000
5.	Sales and Marketing Risk	– 250.000
6.	Financing/Capital Acquisition Risk	+ 0
7.	Competition Risk	-500.000
8.	Technology Risk	+250.000
9.	Litigation Risk	+0
10.	International Risk	-500.000
11.	Reputational Risk	+250.000
12.	Exit Value Risk	-250.000
13.	**Total Adjustment (1 to 12)**	**-500.000**
14.	Average Estimated Value of Comparable Companies in the Sector	5.000.000
15.	**Adjusted Value of the Start-Up Before Capital Acquisition (14 + 13)**	**4.500.000**

Izvor: Walton, 2024a

Problems with the risk factor summation method include its market orientation and the requirement to identify comparable companies within the same geographical location and industry sector, which can be a challenge for newly established companies. The valuation is subject to subjectivity, although the list of analyzed risks is longer and the risk assessment more precise than in the Berkus method.

3.3. Empirical Methods for Valuing Start-Up Companies

3.3.1. The Rule of Thirds Model

The Rule of Thirds model is simple and views a company's value through the lens of three parties: **founders** who have the business idea and contribute capital, **external investors** who invest part of the capital, and **managers** who run the company and often receive shares through equity compensation plans. The Rule of Thirds assumes that each of these three parties holds one-third of the company's equity. After financing, the value of the company equals the post-money valuation, i.e., three times the amount of capital offered by investors. This method is often used by angel investors to quickly value a start-up company. Given its simplicity and arbitrariness, the Rule of Thirds (RoT) is considered more of a valuation tool than a genuine valuation method (Mothersill et al., 2009).

3.3.2. Replacement and Value-Based Balance Sheet Method

The replacement method stems from the cost approach. It estimates the value of the company by considering the cost required to re-establish the same business at the same stage of its life cycle (van de Schootbrugge & Wong, 2013).

The value-based balance sheet method estimates the present value of the company's assets and liabilities while accounting for the level and type of risk (Kallir & Agmon, 2015; Montani, Gervasio & Pulcini, 2020).

The drawbacks of these methods include their inability to consider the future prospects and growth potential of start-ups—factors that are the primary motivation for launching new ventures.

3.3.3. Other Empirical Methods

Empirical methods also include the Berkus method, the scorecard method, and the risk factor summation method, which have been described under qualitative valuation methods.

CONCLUSION

To assess the value of start-up companies, both traditional methods (income, market, and cost approaches) and alternative methods tailored to the specific nature of early-stage businesses can be used. The valuation process for early-stage companies is not linear - it requires a comprehensive evaluation of multiple factors and determinants:

1) Growth potential, profitability of the business idea, and product adaptability;
2) Reliability of the founding team;
3) Success of the product or service prototype;
4) Profitability of the industry sector in which the company operates, as well as the market and competition; and
5) Profit margins.

Therefore, the choice of valuation method for a start-up depends on the characteristics and specific context of the company itself: its stage of development, size, market, industry sector, future growth potential, and the competence of the management team. Given this, there is no single answer as to which valuation method is best for start-ups.

Quantitative alternative valuation methods involve complex procedures, especially in estimating the discount rate or identifying appropriate multiples for comparable companies. Qualitative methods focus on non-financial factors relevant to start-ups, but the valuation of these factors is subject to a high degree of subjectivity.

In general, the discounted cash flow (DCF) method is considered reliable and irreplaceable for valuing both mature and early-stage companies. However, for some start-ups in their earliest stages, due to the lack of historical financial and market data, the DCF method may not be applicable. In such cases, alternative valuation methods should be used.

Valuation methods for start-up companies should reflect their specific characteristics, reduce uncertainty, and ensure a more reliable valuation process. Adequate valuation methods are particularly important in small or developing markets characterized by uncertainty, such as the market in Bosnia and Herzegovina. The most reasonable approach to determining the value of a start-up is to apply several different methods and select the most relevant one within a reasonable range of estimated values.

REFERENCES

Achleitner, A. K., & Lutz, E. (2005). First Chicago Method: Alternative Approach to Valuing Innovative Start-Ups in the Context of Venture Capital Financing Rounds (First-Chicago-Methode-Alternativer Ansatz zur Bewertung von innovativen Unternehmensgründungen bei Venture-Capital-Finanzierungen). *Betriebswirtschaftliche Forschung und Praxis (BFuP), 57*(4), 333-347.

Amis, D., & Stevenson, H.H. (2001). *Winning Angels: The Seven Fundamentals of Early-stage Investing.* Pearson Education.

Babiarz, A. (2016). Methods of valuing investment projects used by Venture Capital funds, financed from public funds. *Prace Naukowe Uniwersytetu Ekonomicznego we Wrocławiu = Research Papers of Wrocław University of Economics, 428*, 11-28. https://doi.org/10.15611/pn.2016.428.01

Babu, A., Arikutaram, C., & Mathews, A. (2023). Risk Factor Summation Method. *A Practical Guide for Startup Valuation.* Springer Nature Switzerland. https://www.springerprofessional.de/en/riskfactorsummationmethod/26086392

Beaton, N. J. (2010). *Valuing early stage and venture-backed companies.* John Wiley & Sons.

Berkus, D. (2012). The Berkus Method–Valuing the Early Stage Investment. *Berkonomics.* https://berkonomics.com/?p=1214

Berkus, D. (2016). After 20 years: Updating the Berkus Method of valuation. *Berkonomics.* https://berkonomics.com/?p=2752

Black, F., & Scholes, M. (1973). The pricing of options and corporate liabilities. *Journal of political economy, 81*(3), 637-654. https://doi.org/10.1086/260062

Copeland, T., Koller T. & Murrin, J. (2000). *Valuation: Measuring and Managing the Value of Companies.* John Wiley and Sons.

Damodaran, A. (2016). *Damodaran on valuation: Security analysis for investment and corporate finance.* John Wiley & Sons.

Damodaran, A. (2002). *Investment Valuation: Tools and Techniques for Determining the Value of Any Asset.* John Wiley and Sons.

Damodaran, A. (2009). *Valuing Young, Start-Up and Growth Companies: Estimation Issues and Valuation Challenges.* Stern School of Business, New York University. https://doi.org/10.2139/ssrn.1418687

Davila, A., & Foster, G. (2005). Management Accounting Systems Adoption Decisions: Evidence and Performance Implications from Early-Stage/Startup Companies. *The Accounting Review, 80*(4), 1039–1068. https://doi.org/10.2308/accr.2005.80.4.1039

Dehghan-Eshratabad, M., & Albadvi, A. (2018). Applying real option approach for startup valuation by venture capitalists in first round of financing. *Management Research in Iran, 22*(3), 1-27.

Demyanova, E. A. (2018). Current issues of company evaluation under fintech. *Strategic decisions and risk management, 1*, 102-117. https://doi.org/10.17747/2078-8886-2018-1-102-1

de Oliveira, F. B., & Zotes, L. P. (2018). Valuation methodologies for business startups: a bibliographical study and survey. *Brazilian Journal of Operations & Production Management, 15*(1), 96-111. https://doi.org/10.14488/BJOPM.2018.v15.n1.a9

Dusatkova, M. S., & Zinecker, M. (2016). Valuing start-ups–selected approaches and their modification based on external factors. *Business: Theory and Practice, 17*, 335. https://doi.org/10.3846/btp.17.11129

Eqvista (2024). *Startup Valuation Methods – How to Value Your Startup?* https://eqvista.com/company-valuation/startup-valuation-methods/

Festel, G., Wuermseher, M., & Cattaneo, G. (2013). Valuation of early stage high-tech start-up companies. *International Journal of Business, 18*(3), 216. https://www.craig.csufresno.edu/ijb/Volumes/Volume%2018/V183-3.pdf

Frykman, D. & Tolleryd, J. (2012). *The Financial Times Guide to Corporate Valuation.* FT Publishing.

Hoseini, S. A., & Moradi Esfanjani, H. (2019). Designing a Valuation Model for Petroleum Startups. *International Journal of Finance & Managerial Accounting, 3*(12), 95-107. http://ijfma.srbiau.ac.ir/article_14029.html

IVSC. (2012). *The Discounted Cash Flow (DCF) Method –Real Property and Business Valuations*. Technical Information Paper 1. IVSC Publishing, London.

Kallir, I., & Agmon, T. (2015). Valuating the Value and Risk of International Start-up Ventures. International *Journal of Financial Research, 6*(2), 203-217. https://doi.org/10.5430/ijfr.v6n2p203

Karius, T. (2016). Intellectual property and intangible assets: Alternative valuation and financing approaches for the knowledge economy in Luxembourg (No. 3). *EIKV-Schriftenreihe zum Wissens-und Wertemanagement*. http://hdl.handle.net/10419/126183

Keeley, R. H., Punjabi, S., & Turki, L. (1996). Valuation of early-stage ventures: option valuation models vs. traditional approaches. *The Journal of Entrepreneurial Finance, 5*(2), 115-138. https://digitalcommons.pepperdine.edu/jef/vol5/iss2/3

Köhn, A. (2018). The determinants of startup valuation in the venture capital context: a systematic review and avenues for future research. *Management Review Quarterly, 68*(1), 3-36. https://doi.org/10.1007/s11301-017-0131-5

Koller, T., Goedhart, M., & Wessels, D. (2020). *Valuation: Measuring and managing the value of companies.* JohnWiley & Sons.

Kollmann, T., Stöckmann, C., Hensellek, S., & Kensbock, J. (2016). *European startup monitor 2016*. Universität Duisburg-Essen Lehrstuhl für E-Business.

Kolvereid, L., & Isaksen, E. (2006). New business start-up and subsequent entry into self-employment. *Journal of Business Venturing, 21*(6), 866-885. https://doi.org/10.1016/j.jbusvent.2005.06.008

Kowlessar F. A. (2016). *The Berkus & Risk Factor Summation Pre-Money Valuation Methods Explained*. https://magazine.startus.cc/berkus-risk-factor-summation-pre-money-valuation-methods-explained/

Laitinen, E. K. (2019). Discounted Cash Flow (DCF) as a Measure of Startup Financial Success. *Theoretical Economics Letters, 9*(08), 2997. https://doi.org/10.4236/tel.2019.98185

Miloud, T., Aspelund, A., & Cabrol, M. (2012). Startup valuation by venture capitalists: an empirical study. *Venture Capital, 14*(2-3), 151-174. https://doi.org/10.1080/13691066.2012.667907

Montani, D., Gervasio, D., & Pulcini, A. (2020). Startup Company Valuation: The State of Art and Future Trends. *International Business Research, 13*(9), 31-45. https://doi.org/10.5539/ibr.v13n9p31

Mothersill, W. D., Watson, B., Fast, F., & Gedeon, S. (2009). *Age of the Angel: Best Practices For Angel Groups*. National Angel Organization, Canada.

Payne, B. (2011a). *Scorecard Valuation Methodology. Establishing the Valuation of Prerevenue, Startup Companies*. https://www.semanticscholar.org/paper/SCORECARDVALUATIONMETHODOLOGYEstablishingtheofPayne/e97709f963bf19d548d9e7dc8fdb30610717dae6

Payne, B. (2011b). *Valuations 101: The Risk Factor Summation Method.* http://blog.gust.com/valuations-101-the-risk-factor-summation-method/

Reis, P., & Augusto, M. (2013). The terminal value (TV) performing in firm valuation: The gap of literature and research agenda. *Journal of Modern Accounting and Auditing, 9*(12), 1622-1636. http://hdl.handle.net/10400.19/3621

Rose, D. S. (2014). *Angel investing: The gust guide to making money and having fun investing in startups*. John Wiley & Sons.

Rotich, R. (2024). *10 Effective Startup Valuation Methods and Why They Work.* https://www.indeed.com/career-advice/career-development/startup-valuation-methods

Sahlman, W. A., & Scherlis, D. R. (1987). A Method for Valuing High-Risk, Long-Term Investments: The Venture Capital Method. *Harvard Business School Background Note 288-006*. https://www.hbs.edu/faculty/Pages/item.aspx?num=6515

Serdar Raković, T. (2020). *Assessment of the Company Value. Review of Inactive Capital Markets*. Faculty of Economics, University of Banja Luka.

Shestakov, D. (2015). Real Option Approach to Evaluate Strategic Flexibility for Startup Projects. In Cobanoglu & Ongan, Eds., *Proceedings of the International Interdisciplinary Business and Economics Conference: Volume 3* (pp.360-368). https://doi.org/10.5038/2372-5885-v3

van de Schootbrugge, E., & Wong, K. M. (2013). Multi-Stage Valuation for Start-Up High Tech Projects and Companies. *Journal of Accounting and Finance, 13*(2), 45-56.

Walton, C. JD. (2024a). *Startup Valuation: 10 Methods, Factors & Best Practices.* Eton Venture Services. https://etonvs.com/valuation/startup-valuation/

Walton, C. JD. (2024b). *How to Value a Startup Company with No Revenue – 3 Ways.* https://etonvs.com/valuation/how-to-value-a-startup-company-with-no-revenue/

Wardani, I. S., & Fujiwara, T. (2018). Applying a Two-Stage Option Games Method to Investment Decisions of Business Startups: Case Study of a Smart House Startup in Indonesia. *Asian Journal of Innovation and Policy, 7*(1), 178-189.

CLOSING NOTE

The papers compiled in this volume reflect a sustained engagement with the core challenges of business valuation in transitional and emerging markets. While each chapter addresses a distinct issue, ranging from the construction of the discount rate to the implications of market liquidity -the collection as a whole underscores the broader methodological and contextual complexities that define valuation practice in such environments.

Rather than offering definitive conclusions, the volume seeks to illuminate the evolving nature of valuation theory and application. By presenting both theoretical developments and empirical evidence across a defined period, it offers insight into the progression of thought within a dynamic academic and regulatory landscape.

It is hoped that this compilation will serve not only as a resource for further study but also as a foundation for continued dialogue and research. The enduring relevance of these topics attests to the necessity of ongoing inquiry, critical reflection, and methodological rigor in the field of corporate finance.

www.ingramcontent.com/pod-product-compliance
Lightning Source LLC
LaVergne TN
LVHW022058200926
848481LV00003B/978
* 9 7 9 8 8 9 9 6 6 2 3 6 2 *